Peggy Love's Cook Book

Have Fun While You Cook!

by

Peggy Love

Bless, O Lord,
These delectable vittles,
May they add to thy glory,
And not to our middles!

Enjoy —
Peggy Anderson

AuthorHouse - rev. 12/6/06

Recipe Index

From Peggy Love

Dedication

Peggy Love Mitchell Anderson, is my real name, but over the years, my husband, Vic, has just called me "Peggy Love". In our fifty years together, Vic has been my strength, my love, and my best friend. So, it is to him that I affectionately dedicate this book. (Plus, he loves my cooking)

Introduction

Welcome to our family cookbook. Let me introduce you to my family: I have two handsome sons, Victor and Mitch, and two lovely daughters, Donna and Carol, and of course my faithful husband of fifty years, Vic.

In July of the year 2000, we celebrated our 50th Wedding Anniversary. We found the "recipe" for sharing and caring! I hope you are so blessed.

Added to this, is daughter-in-law Linda, and son-in-laws Paul and Mark H. Also as you might expect I have been blessed with six fantastic grandchildren: Tori, Karen, Justin, Ashley, Victor IV (orV4), and Michael plus two great grandsons, Kaleb and Gage.

I want to thank all of my family for help in completing this cookbook, with a special thanks to my son-in-law Paul, for putting this all together.

My family is very important to me and in this book you will see their names included many times. Over the years I have collected many excellent recipes and had adventures you would not believe.

I'd like to share not only my recipes with you, but also many of our family stories. Hopefully, the combination will make this cookbook a little different than most. As your food is bubbling on the stove, you can read about our life and maybe add a smile to your day.

I've also included a *"Mind Snacks"* section on most pages. People often like to snack while they cook. You won't gain weight with these "mind snacks". Well, let's get to it...

50th Anniversary Special

In the year 2000 Vic and I celebrated our 50th Wedding anniversary. Our family informed us that they had something special planned for us. They asked us to reserve a week in July and told us we'd get more specific details later.

Well as promised, as we approached the week in July we got instructions on what to pack and were told we would be delivered to the airport (destination unknown).

As scheduled, when the week arrived, a friend of the family delivered us to LAX and placed tickets in our hands to Aruba! As we checked in with the ticket Agent I couldn't help sharing that we were going to Aruba as a gift from our family for our 50'th Anniversary. She said, "Oh that's wonderful. What a coincidence. We had a whole bunch of Anderson's flying to Aruba last night."

Vic and I looked at each other and then back to the ticket Agent. She slowly turned red as she realized she had spoken out of turn and may have shared a bit too much information.

When we arrived in Aruba we were met at the airport by a nice lady carrying a sign with our names on it. She drove us across Aruba and up the beach and pulled into a beautiful home located right on the beach.

As we walked up to the house our entire family poured out of the house, surrounding us, showering us with hugs and kisses. What a wonderful feeling and how precious family is.

The house was located on the beach at a prime snorkeling location and had a walled area in back with a huge pool, Jacuzzi, gazebo, etc.

We had a very memorably week. We went snorkeling, scuba diving, hang-gliding, went on a Submarine, rented Jeeps and drove all over the Island, and spent evening after evening watching the sun go down over the ocean.

When you are young, you spend so much time nurturing and giving of yourself to your family. If you are lucky, some day your family "gives" back to you. We have been very lucky!

Appetizers

Tired of serving the same things all the time?

There are probably a few recipes here you have not tried.

They're all so easy!

All of these recipes may be served at a morning coffee, afternoon tea, appetizers before a meal, or for a cocktail party. They're bound to be a hit!

Great appetizers are the beginning of great social evenings.

Or, of course, if a neighbor drops by in the afternoon.

Or just for you and your family to enjoy.

All of these are our family favorites.

Hope you enjoy serving them also.

Asparagus Roll-Ups

This one is a lot of work but is worth it.

- ♥ 16 fresh asparagus spears
- ♥ 16 slices of sandwich bread with crust removed
- ♥ 1 package of 8 ounce cream cheese (softened)
- ♥ 8 bacon strips cooked and crumbled
- ♥ 2 tablespoons minced chives
- ♥ ¼ cup butter melted
- ♥ 3 tablespoons grated parmesan cheese

Place asparagus in skillet with a small amount of water.

Cook until tender and set aside.

Flatten bread with a rolling pin.

Combine cream cheese, bacon, and chives.

Spread 1 tablespoon of cream cheese mixture on each flattened bread slice.

Place an asparagus spear on each bread slice and roll up tightly.
Place each roll on a greased baking dish with the seam side down.

Brush with butter and sprinkle with Parmesan.

Cut roll-ups in half and bake at 400 degrees for 10-12 minutes.

Mind Snacks!

- ♥ A lie can travel halfway around the world while truth is putting on its shoes. *(Mark Twain)*

- ♥ The mind, like machinery, rusts from idleness.

Avocado Dip

Very different. Serve to your more adventurous friends.

- ♥ 2 peeled, pitted, ripe avocados
- ♥ 1 cup sour cream
- ♥ ½ tsp. Salt
- ♥ 2 tablespoons horseradish
- ♥ 1 grated small onion

With electric mixer, mash avocados to smooth paste.

Add rest of ingredients.

Beat well.

Chill.

Serve with chips.

Mind Snacks!

- ♥ A little boy's prayer; God Bless Mom, God Bless Dad, God Bless Grandmom, and please take care of yourself God, cause if anything happens to you we are all sunk.

- ♥ A child on a farm sees a plane fly overhead and dreams of faraway places. A traveler on the plane sees the farmhouse and dreams of home.

- ♥ To be successful; Know what you are doing, Love what you are doing, and believe in what you are doing.

Bean Dip

A very tasty Mexican appetizer.

- ♥ 1/3 cup sour cream
- ♥ 8 oz. cream cheese
- ♥ 4 oz. shredded jack cheese
- ♥ 4 oz. shredded cheddar cheese
- ♥ small can bean dip
- ♥ ½ pkg. Taco seasoning mix

Blend ingredients and serve with Doritos.

Mind Snacks!

- ♥ If your baby is beautiful and perfect, never cries or fusses, sleeps on schedule and burps on demand, and is an angel all the time…. You're the grandmother!

- ♥ Only man has been given the privilege and the means to fix his own habits.

- ♥ Ideas are like rabbits. You get a couple and learn how to handle them, and pretty soon you have a dozen.

- ♥ The older I get…the better I was.

- ♥ If you have time for idle gossip, you're probably too busy for success.

Benedictine Dip

Something different.

Nice for Christmas (its green)!

- ♥ 8 oz. sour cream or cream cheese
- ♥ 1 large cucumber, minced
- ♥ 1 medium onion, minced
- ♥ 1 tablespoon mayonnaise
- ♥ 2 drops green food coloring

Beat cream cheese until smooth.

Stir in remaining ingredients.

Blend well.

Chill and serve with chips.

Mind Snacks!

- ♥ You don't stop laughing because you grow old. You grow old because you stop laughing.
- ♥ To have a friend you have to be a friend.
- ♥ The road to success is always under construction.
- ♥ He never gets much done who starts tomorrow.
- ♥ Listening may be the sincerest form of flattery.

Bridge Mix

All kids from 6 - 90 love this snack!

- ♥ 1 cup Wheat Chex
- ♥ 1 cup Rice Chex
- ♥ 1 cup Cherios
- ♥ 1 cup pretzels
- ♥ 1 cup pecan halves
- ♥ 1 tablespoon Worcestershire sauce
- ♥ 1 tablespoon garlic salt
- ♥ 1/3 cup butter

Melt butter in shallow pan.

Add all ingredients.

Bake 250 degrees for 45 minutes turning every 10 minutes.

Drain on paper towels.

Mind Snacks!

- ♥ The world is happier when people laugh together.
- ♥ Every adult needs a child to teach, which is the way adults learn.
- ♥ People tend to talk more than they have something to say.
- ♥ Excuses are the nails used to build a house of failure.
- ♥ Democracy does not guarantee equality, only equality of opportunity.

Broccoli - Cheese Dip

I have a dip for every taste!

- ♥ 1 can broccoli cheese soup
- ♥ 1 package frozen chopped broccoli (thawed and drained)
- ♥ 1 medium tomato (chopped)
- ♥ ½ cup sour cream
- ♥ 2 teaspoons Dijon mustard

Mix ingredients and chill.

Server with assorted crackers.

Mind Snacks!

- ♥ When the going seems easy, check to make sure you are not coasting.

- ♥ Getting people to like you is only the other side of liking them.

- ♥ Any child can tell you that the sole purpose of a middle name is so he can tell when he is really in trouble.

- ♥ Drop the word "impossible" from your vocabulary.

- ♥ A lie has speed but truth has endurance.

Carol's Cheese Ball

The best cheese ball ever.
Unless you are having company, cut the recipe in half.

- ♥ 2 - 8 ½ oz cream cheese packages
- ♥ 1 - 8 oz. can crushed pineapple (drain & pat with paper towel)
- ♥ ¼ cup diced green peppers
- ♥ 2 tablespoons minced onion
- ♥ 1 tablespoons seasoned salt
- ♥ 1 cup chopped pecans (save some to roll ball in)

Form into two balls and roll in pecans.

Chill and serve (and enjoy).

Mind Snacks!

- ♥ A man chases a woman until she catches him.

- ♥ What we must decide is how we are valuable rather than how valuable we are.

- ♥ When one is out of touch with oneself, one cannot touch others.

- ♥ One thing that gets the goat of an angry person is a smile when he expects a frown.

We Meet Brendie

When we lived in Kentucky we had a beagle, two cats, and took in a Great Dane. His master had died and she was so distraught that she moped around all day so we agreed to make her part of our family.

Her name was Brendie and she was a very large dog. She accepted us quickly and became part of our family. She was very well trained so we kept her in the house all the time. She would race through the house, never touching anything.

On one occasion I had been gone for a couple of hours and when I returned I found an antique lamp lying broken on the floor. My two boys, ages 4 and 14 told me immediately that Brendie had broken it. Of course before the end of the day I learned that the boys had been playing in the "off limits" living room and had broken it. They thought they could get off the hook by blaming Brendie.

Mind Snacks!

♥ Everybody thinks of changing humanity and nobody thinks of changing himself. *(Leo Tolstoy)*

♥ We may not return the affection of those who like us, but we always respect their good judgment.

♥ Every young man has to learn to paddle his own canoe, even if his father owns a yacht.

Margaret's Cheese Dip

Serve with vegetables or crackers.

A real favorite with any crowd.

- ♥ 2 - 8 oz. Cream cheese
- ♥ grate ½ small onion
- ♥ ½ cup tomato catsup
- ♥ 8 drops Tabasco
- ♥ 1 T. Worcestershire sauce

Blend in blender.

Chill.

Serve with chips or vegetables.

Brendie's Bell

In Kentucky we lived out a little ways from town and in the back of our house was a farm. After the school bus left in the morning, I would let our Great Dane Brendie out and she would run and do her "business" out on the farm.

Then she would run and play. After a while she would come up on the back porch and ring the doorbell and I would let her in.

She would then watch TV until the kids came home from school.

Chicken Fingers with Honey Mustard

Surprise your family with chicken fingers that taste a lot different than frozen.

- ♥ 4 skinless boneless chicken breasts
- ♥ bowl of milk (big enough to dip chicken breasts)
- ♥ flour mixed with salt and pepper to taste

Dip chicken in milk and roll in flour mixture.

Fry until brown and crispy in vegetable oil.

Drain on paper towels.

Cut chicken breasts in small pieces.

Serve with honey mustard.

Easier than you thought, isn't it.

Mind Snacks!

- ♥ When the going is hardest, just put on a smile and you'll get there sooner.
- ♥ We are all mortals until the first kiss and the second glass of wine.
- ♥ The world makes room for people who know where they are going.
- ♥ Find a job you love and you'll never have to work a day in your life.

Chili Cheese Log

Especially good for parties.

Quite different.

- ♥ ¾ lb. Grated American cheese
- ♥ 1 - 3 oz. package soft cream cheese
- ♥ ¼ tsp. Salt
- ♥ 1 ½ tsp. Worcestershire sauce
- ♥ Chili powder (to taste)

Thoroughly combine all ingredients except chili powder with mixer.

Shape in 2 thin logs.

Sprinkle chili powder on wax paper.

Roll each log in chili power coating evenly.

Wrap in wax paper and chill.

Slice and serve with assorted crackers.

Mind Snacks!

♥ In the long run men hit only what they aim at.

♥ The most important things in life aren't things.

♥ If you can play golf and bridge as though they were games, you're just about as well adjusted as you are ever going to be.

A Sad Goodbye

In 1979 Vic's company wanted us to move to California. We knew we could not handle a big dog in California and Brendie needed room to run.

We found a friend of a friend who wanted her and agreed to make their home hers. They had no children and would be "loving parents".

The night before we left my youngest son Mitch spent the night with these "strangers to him" to make sure they loved Brendie and would take care of her. His dog was more important to him than spending his last night with his friends.

About five years later we heard of a girl in Brendie's new neighborhood who had married and had a baby girl whom she name Brendie!

Mind Snacks!

♥ The hardest thing to learn in life is which bridge to cross and which to burn.

♥ In order to maintain a well-balanced perspective, the person who has a dog to worship him should also have a cat to ignore him.

♥ Reason deceives us, conscience, never.

Cocktail Hot Dogs

Kids and adults alike love this. Warms the tummy!

- ¾ cup prepared mustard
- 1 - (1 ounce jar) current jelly

Mix and heat.

Slice 1 pound of hot dogs and add to mixture.

Serve with toothpicks.

Mind Snacks!

- It requires wisdom to understand wisdom; the music is nothing if the audience is deaf.

- Everyone is a fool for at least five minutes every day. Wisdom consists in not exceeding the limit.

- Wisdom is the quality that keeps you from getting into situations where you need it.

- The young man knows the rules, but the old man knows the exceptions.

- You're never too old to grow up.

Breakfast in Bed!

In the summer of 1959 Vic had to go to Chicago on business. He took the three kids and me with him. We were so excited. The only vacations we took were business trips, which usually consisted of one or two nights in a motel. We had never stayed in a hotel with the kids.

When the great day arrived, off we went. On all our trips with the kids, what we mostly did was answer their questions. This trip was no exception.

We stayed at the Sheraton Hotel in Chicago. We checked in, had dinner, and went to our connecting rooms. With the door open we settled the kids into their beds in their room.

Carol, who was 4 years old at that time, asked excitedly, "I wonder what they'll serve us for breakfast in bed". The other kids laughed at her and stated, in their infinite wisdom, "Just because you stay in a hotel does not mean they serve you breakfast in bed"!

Carol, affronted, asserted, "Yes they do!" She had seen them do it on our recently acquired TV set at home. Vic overheard this conversation and with a slight smile on his face and a twinkle in his eye, he very quietly called room service and ordered breakfast in bed for 8 am.

Carol is still saying "I told you so"! I'm glad we stayed only one night because we couldn't afford another "breakfast in bed".

Mind Snacks!

♥ Cooperation is doing with a smile what you have to do anyway.

♥ As we grow old, the beauty steals inward. *(Ralph Waldo Emerson)*

♥ A man without a purpose is as helpless as a ship without a compass.

Corn and Ham Quiche

Use oblong Pyrex dish.

- ♥ 1 can sweet corn, drained
- ♥ 1 finely chopped onion
- ♥ ¾ cup sour cream
- ♥ 3 eggs
- ♥ 4 ounces chopped ham
- ♥ 3 ounces grated cheddar cheese
- ♥ ½ cup milk
- ♥ pie crust

Press pie crust into bottom of dish.

Mix corn, ham, onion, & cheese together.

Spread over crust.

Beat together sour cream, milk, & eggs.

Pour this mixture over corn mixture.

Bake 350 degrees for 30 minutes (until top is golden and filling is firm).

Let cool and cut into squares to serve.

Mind Snacks!

- ♥ You will never be as happy as when you know you are making someone else happy.

- ♥ The nice thing about egotists is that they don't talk about other people.

- ♥ If it isn't your job, perhaps it's your opportunity.

Cottage Cheese Dip

Something a little different.

- ♥ 1 cup small curd cottage cheese
- ♥ ¼ cup creamy cucumber dressing
- ♥ 2 tablespoons green onions (chopped fine)
- ♥ 3 slices bacon (cooked crisp and crumbled)
- ♥ 1 tablespoon pimento minced

Combine all ingredients.

Mix well and chill.

Serve with chips or raw vegetables.

Mind Snacks!

- ♥ An attractive personality is a personality that attracts.
- ♥ Praise in public, Criticize in private.
- ♥ Initiative is doing the right thing without being told.
- ♥ A hug is a great gift. One size fits all and it is easy to exchange.
- ♥ Take care of your reputation. It is your most valuable asset.
- ♥ Every once in a while take the scenic route.

Crabmeat Canapés

Sweet and crunchy!

- ♥ 1 - 6 ounce can crabmeat
- ♥ 2 teaspoons mayonnaise
- ♥ Melba toast
- ♥ 1 teaspoon grated onion
- ♥ ½ cup grated cheddar cheese

Flake crabmeat and toss with mayonnaise and onion.

Spoon on Melba toast.

Sprinkle generously with cheese.

Broil 1 to 2 minutes until cheese is melted and slightly browned.

Serve hot.

Mind Snacks!

- ♥ A man without enthusiasm is like an automobile without gas.

- ♥ Be a leader: Remember the lead sled dog is the only one with a decent view.

- ♥ As a general rule the most successful man in life is the man who has the best information.

Deviled Ham Balls

These will go quickly.

- ♥ 3 - 2 ½ ounce cans of deviled ham
- ♥ ¼ cup pretzels coarsely crushed
- ♥ dash of pepper
- ♥ 8 ounces cream cheese (soft)

Form into 25 small balls and freeze 20 minutes.

Roll each ball in tablespoon cream cheese to cover.

Roll in chives if desired.

Refrigerate.

Mind Snacks!

- ♥ You can't make a place for yourself in the sun if you keep sitting in the shade of the family tree.

- ♥ Any jackass can kick a barn down…It takes a carpenter to rebuild it.

- ♥ Why not go out on a limb? Isn't that where the fruit is?

- ♥ Laughter is the jam on the toast of life. It adds flavor, keeps it from being too dry, and makes it easier to swallow.

Fruit Dip #1

Very tasty.

- ♥ 1 cup orange juice
- ♥ 2 tablespoons cornstarch
- ♥ 1 cup sugar
- ♥ 1 cup pineapple juice

Mix together and cook until thick, stirring constantly. Let cool and fold in ½ pint whipping cream. Serve with fresh fruit of your choice.

Mind Snacks!

- ♥ Don't make love by the garden gate. Love is blind, but the neighbors ain't!

- ♥ We don't believe in rheumatism and true love until after the first attack.

- ♥ Two things only a man cannot hide: that he is drunk and that he is in love.

- ♥ Only love can be divided endlessly and still not diminish.

- ♥ A baby is born with a need to be loved - and never outgrows it.

Fruit Dip #2

The easy fruit dip.

- ♥ 2 cups marshmallow crème
- ♥ 2 cups mayonnaise

Blend together and serve with fresh fruit as a dip.

Mind Snacks!

- ♥ Midlife crisis is that moment when you realize your children and your clothes are about the same age.

- ♥ Count memories like money.

- ♥ When I was younger, I could remember anything, whether it had happened or not. *(Mark Twain)*

- ♥ You never know when you're making a memory.

- ♥ Anything we can dream we can do.

- ♥ If a man had as many ideas during the day as he does when he has insomnia, he'd make a fortune.

- ♥ Plant and your spouse plants with you, weed and you weed alone.

Friendly Updraft

Vic and I had only been married 2 years when the company wanted to send him to New York for a business meeting. Another salesman with the company, named Tom would also be going.

This was the early 1950's. At that time women didn't wear pants in public. Harriet played the organ at the Methodist church and Tom sang in the choir and also did barbershop singing. They were very devout and nice people. They were a few years older than we were. I was 22.

While in New York we decided to go to Coney Island. I'm not much on rides. They often make me sick. Well of course the first thing they wanted to do was ride the "parachute". You sat in the seat, take a ride high up to the top, drop a few feet fast, the parachute opens, and you drift slowly down. I let them talk me into riding this thing.

Well I got sick and Harriet had enough, so we sent the men off to play on the remaining rides and we women sat down in some seats in front of a stage to wait for them. Well we soon got a show!

Clowns appeared on stage and people started to gather. Some women came through a door and their skirts blew up around their ears. Harriet and I watched people come out that door with all the women having the same thing happen. We wondered what kind of women would put themselves in that position. We called them "low class"!

Well, the men came to pick us up and laughed at the people getting blasted as they came through the doorway. Soon we decided to leave. On our way out the men saw another ride they wanted to go on and it seemed pretty mild so we agreed. It was wooden horses that went around a large track and only went as fast as you pedaled.

It was a long ride and we thought it would never end. It wound its way through the whole park and finally ended quite a ways from where we got on. We got off the ride and exited through a doorway and as my skirt blew up around my ears, I knew exactly where we were!

Grape Appetizers

Pretty, great tasting, and very good as a garnish!

- ♥ Stem, wash, & dry seedless green grapes.
- ♥ Split each one open and stuff with softened cream cheese.
- ♥ Toast slivered almonds until lightly brown.
- ♥ Dip stuffed grapes in nuts.

This recipe is work, but it is worth it!

Mind Snacks!

- ♥ Some folks never exaggerate - they just remember big.

- ♥ The older a man gets, the farther he had to walk to school as a boy.

- ♥ If you're yearning for the good old days, just turn off the air conditioning.

- ♥ Things ain't what they used to be and probably never was.

- ♥ Home is a place you grow up wanting to leave, and grow old wanting to get back to.

Sing a Song

Some friends of ours, Lois and Steve, love to travel but they will not fly. We like to meet them and take a week of "sight seeing" in our car.

One year we flew to Denver and they picked us up and we went north through the Tetons. We went all the way up to Vancouver and to British Columbia. What a magnificent trip! Beauty beyond belief!

We stopped at Lake Louise, arriving about 10:30 in the morning to see the sights and have lunch overlooking the lake, but to our disappointment they were closing for the winter and lunch would not be served.

All the guests that were in the lobby joined hands, including us, and sang "Auld Lang Syne".

What an experience. Its something we will never forget.

Mind Snacks!

- ♥ Be slow in choosing a friend, slower in changing. *(Benjamin Franklin)*

- ♥ We need old friends to help us grow old and new friends to help us stay young.

- ♥ A friend is someone you can do nothing with, and enjoy it.

- ♥ A true friend never gets in your way unless you happen to be going down.

Guacamole Dip

Another great dish for your Mexican fiesta celebrations.

- ♥ 1 medium ripe avocado (halved, seeded, and peeled)
- ♥ 4 ½ teaspoon lemon or lime juice
- ♥ 1 small tomato finely chopped
- ♥ ½ cup finely chopped onions
- ♥ 1 garlic clove minced

Mash avocado with the lemon or lime juice.

Stir in tomatoes, onions, and garlic.

Cover and chill.

Serve with tortilla chips.

If you make this ahead of time put seed of avocado on top of dip and cover to keep fresh. (Don't forget to remove the seed before serving!)

Mind Snacks!

♥ Dieters prayer for the Holidays:
Lord, grant me the strength that I may not fall,
Into the clutches of cholesterol,
At polyunsaturates I'll never mutter,
For the road to hell is paved with butter,
And cake is cursed, and cream is awful,
And Satan is hiding in every waffle,
Beelzebub is a chocolate drop,
Lucifer is a lollipop,
Teach me the evils of hollandaise,
Of pasta, and gobs of mayonnaise,
And crisp, fried chicken from the south,
Lord if you love me, shut my mouth!

Hot Artichoke Dip

Impress your guests with this seemingly fancy delight!

- ♥ 1 cup parmesan cheese
- ♥ 1 cup mayonnaise
- ♥ 1 cup artichoke hearts

Drain and dice artichoke hearts.

Mix all ingredients.

Bake 350 degrees until top bubbles and browns.

Serve hot with crackers.

Mind Snacks!

- ♥ Pay attention to your enemies for they are the first to discover your mistakes.

- ♥ Great opportunities to help others seldom come, but small ones surround us every day.

- ♥ You may give gifts without caring - but you can't care without giving.

- ♥ We'd all like a reputation for generosity, and we'd all like to buy it cheap.

- ♥ Real charity doesn't care if its tax deductible or not. *(Dan Bennett)*

Times Have Changed

At the end of a trip with our friends Lois and Steve, they dropped us off in Seattle and left to drive down the West Coast. It was 3:00 in the afternoon and we were uncertain what to do.

We discovered that the Seattle basketball team was playing the Portland team at the old world's fair site and we decided to go. It was suggested to us that we should take the hotel limo to downtown Seattle and then take the monorail out to the game. We did and everything went like clockwork.

We had good seats at the game and at half time Vic went out exploring. As I sat waiting one of the ushers came over to talk to me. I told him our life story (the short version). He asked how we were going to return to the hotel. I said the same way we came.

He said the monorail closed at 8 p.m. and there were no taxis to get us to downtown Seattle. We had a problem. The usher suggested we meet him at gate 2 after the game ended and he would drop us off as he went right by our hotel. I agreed without giving it another thought.

Later, when we went to his vehicle we found it was a camper truck. We got leery immediately, but he took us straight to our hotel and would not take a dime for his trouble. We wouldn't dream of doing that today!

<table>
<tr><td>Mind Snacks!</td></tr>
</table>

♥ The difference between a helping hand and an outstretched palm is a twist of the wrist.

♥ Old is always fifteen years from now.

Hot Brie Cheese

This is absolutely great!

- ♥ Use a wedge of Brie cheese, put slivered almonds on top.
- ♥ Heat in microwave until hot. DO NOT LET IT MELT!

Serve it with crackers or for something really special serve with tart green apples.

Mind Snacks!

- ♥ God has given us two ears and one mouth so that we can listen twice as much as we speak.

- ♥ The best way to get rid of an enemy is to make him a friend.

- ♥ Of all the things you wear, your expression is the most important.

- ♥ Common sense is the knack of seeing things as they are, and then doing the right thing about it.

- ♥ A rich man once asked a friend, "Why am I criticized for being miserly? Everyone knows I will leave everything to charity when I die'. "Well," said the friend, "Let me tell you about the pig and the cow." The pig was lamenting to the cow one day about how unpopular he was. "People are always talking about your gentleness and your kind eyes," said the pig. "Sure, you give milk and cream, but I give more. I give bacon, ham, loins, then even pickle my feet. Still nobody likes me. Why is this?" The cow thought a minute then replied, "Well, maybe it's because I give while I'm still living."

Hot Cheese Balls

Great for morning coffee or afternoon teas.

Prepare this and keep in the freezer to bake when you need something quick.

- ♥ 1 cup sharp cheddar cheese, grated
- ♥ 1 cup flour
- ♥ 1 cup rice krispies
- ♥ 1 stick soft butter

Mix together and form into small balls.

Bake 350 degrees for 7 minutes.

Flatten with fork and bake another two minutes.

May be frozen before baking.

Mind Snacks!

Ever notice:

- ♥ That when someone asks if you have a minute, he's really asking for 20.

- ♥ Or no matter how many TV channels you switch to you always get a commercial.

- ♥ That a parking meter is the only place where you can literally buy time.

- ♥ That the world is full of people who go through life running from something that isn't chasing them.

- ♥ That you spend 18 months trying to get your children to stand up and talk and the next 18 years trying to get them to sit down and listen.

In-Ter-Peed!

Each Christmas the whole family gets together and has an adventure. Many interesting and funny things happen on these adventures.

We usually rent an extra car or two so the kids can take off on their own and do things.

One year, my son-in-law Mark, kept referring to something called an In-Ter-Peed (in phonetic form). He would say, "Wait here and I'll go get the In-Ter-Peed". Then he would pick up us in the rental car that was assigned to him.

Everywhere we went it was the same. We all looked at each and occasionally chuckled. Finally, we had to ask. What was this mysterious In-Ter-Peed he kept referring to.

Well, of course, it was the rental car; a Dodge In-Ter-Peed, more commonly known as a Dodge Intrepid.

Mind Snacks!

♥   The value of marriage is not that adults produce children, but that children produce adults.

♥   Whoever thinks marriage is a 50-50 proposition doesn't know the half of it.

♥   Getting married is easy. Staying married is more difficult. Staying happily married for a lifetime should rank among the fine arts.

Olive Cheese Ball

Very near the top on my favorite list!

- ♥ 1 - 8 oz. package soft cream cheese
- ♥ 4 oz. grated cheddar cheese
- ♥ ¼ cup soft oleo
- ♥ 2/3 cup chopped ripe green olives
- ♥ 1 tablespoon minced chives
- ♥ 1/3 cup finely chopped walnuts

Blend cheese and oleo until smooth.

Stir in olives and chives.

Shape into 2 balls.

Coat with walnuts.

Chill.

Devour!

Mind Snacks!

♥ A pessimist is someone who complains about the noise when opportunity knocks.

♥ Benjamin Franklin:

If you would not be forgotten,

As soon as you are dead and rotten,

Either write things worth reading,

Or do things worth the writing.

♥ Real love stories never have endings.

Oyster Cracker Snack

Great for people who are watching their diets.

No cholesterol.

- ♥ 1 - 12 oz. package of oyster crackers
  (low sodium - no cholesterol)
- ♥ 1 package original ranch style dressing mix
- ♥ ½ cup oil

Put crackers in large bowl.

Pour oil over crackers.

Sprinkle dressing mix over all.

Let stand about 30 minutes.

Store in tins.

Mind Snacks!

- ♥ Success is never final, but failure can be.

- ♥ You are never fully dressed unless you wear a smile.

- ♥ A man complained to his barber that his hairline seemed to be receding and that there was a worrisome thinning in front. "A bald forehead means you're a thinker", said the barber. The man liked that but wondered aloud about the top spot. "That means you're a lover", he replied. The man was feeling good until the barber added, "Of course, if you lose hair in the front and on top, that means you only think you're a lover".

Ranch Meat Balls

Quick and tasty for the meat lovers!

- ♥ 1 packet original ranch dressing mix
- ♥ 1 pound ground beef
- ♥ 2 tablespoons butter
- ♥ ½ cup beef broth

Combine ground beef and dressing mixture.

Shape into meatballs.

Melt butter in a skillet and brown on both sides.

Add broth.

Cover and simmer until cooked through (10-15 minutes).

Serve warm with toothpicks.

Mind Snacks!

- ♥ When enthusiasm comes in the front door, worry runs out the back door.

- ♥ The reason people blame things on previous generations is that there is only one other choice.

- ♥ What we do during our working hours determines what we have; What we do in our leisure hours determines what we are.

- ♥ Often the difference between a successful marriage and a mediocre one consists of about 3 or 4 things a day left unsaid.

- ♥ We never know the love of the parent until we become parents ourselves.

Sausage Balls *(the easy way)*

These you can keep frozen and bake when company pops in.

- ♥ 1 pound mild sausage
- ♥ 1 - 8 ounce jar cheez whiz
- ♥ 1 ½ cup bisquick

Mix with hands.

Roll into small balls.

Bake at 400 degrees for 20 minutes.

Mind Snacks!

- ♥ Start going the extra mile and opportunity will start following you.

- ♥ Experience: Experience is a wonderful thing. It enables you to recognize a mistake when you make it again.

- ♥ Optimism: An optimist is someone who tells you to cheer up when things are going his way.

- ♥ Adolescence is perhaps nature's way of preparing parents to welcome the empty nest.

- ♥ Few things are more satisfying than seeing your children have teenagers of their own.

- ♥ The most important thing a father can do for his children to love their mother.

Spiced Pineapple Pick-Ups

Great served anytime, with anything, but especially nice for an "extra" at parties!

So nice because you can make this one 2 or 3 days ahead of time.

- ♥ 1 large can pineapple chunks
- ♥ ¾ cup vinegar
- ♥ 1 ½ cup sugar
- ♥ dash salt
- ♥ 6 whole cloves
- ♥ 1 - 4 inch stick cinnamon

2 days ahead, drain syrup from pineapple.

Add next 5 ingredients.

Heat 10 minutes.

Add pineapple.

Bring to boil.

Remove from heat and refrigerate.

To serve: drain pineapple. Serve with toothpicks.

Mind Snacks!

- ♥ Age does not protect you from love, but love protects you from old age.

- ♥ Fame changes a lot of things, but it can't change a light bulb.

- ♥ My father didn't tell me how to live; he lived, and let me watch him do it.

Stuffed Cherry Tomatoes #1

Looks good! Tastes good! Great as a garnish!

- ♥ 40 cherry tomatoes
  Mix together:
- ♥ 2/3 cup celery
- ♥ 3 tablespoons onions, minced
- ♥ 3 tablespoons wine vinegar
- ♥ dash salt
- ♥ 1 tsp. sugar

Scoop out tomatoes and fill. Chill 2 hours.

Mind Snacks!

- ♥ Your worst humiliation is someone's momentary entertainment.
- ♥ The simplest toy, one which even the youngest child can operate, is called a grandparent.

  (Sam Levenson)
- ♥ If you want your children to keep their feet on the ground, put some responsibility on their shoulders.
- ♥ A truly rich man is one whose children run in his arms when his hands are empty.
- ♥ Trust yourself. You know more than you think you do. *(Benjamin Spock, MD)*
- ♥ There are lots of people who mistake their imagination for their memory.

Peek-A-Boo Television

When our daughter Donna was 2 years old we started having trouble getting her to go to bed. She wanted to stay up and watch television. Donna, with her own personal flair, was very insistent.

To get her into bed, we would pretend to go to bed when we put her down. Then when she was asleep we would quietly get back up and watch television.

What we didn't know until later is that she was pretending to go to sleep and quietly getting up and sitting in the kitchen, peeking around the door, and watching television with us.

When we started to get ready for bed she would scramble back to bed and be sound asleep when I checked on her.

We didn't find out until a couple of years later when we found her asleep on the kitchen floor!

Mind Snacks!

♥ If you can't hold children in your arms, please hold them in your heart.

♥ Never insult an alligator until after you have crossed the river.

♥ No man knows his true character until he has run out of gas, purchased something on the installment plan, and raised an adolescent.

Stuffed Cherry Tomatoes #2

Great tasting and beautiful as a garnish.

- ♥ 1 pint cherry tomatoes
- ♥ 4 ounces crumbled blue cheese
- ♥ ½ cup finely chopped red onion
- ♥ ½ cup vegetable oil
- ♥ ¼ cup red wine vinegar
- ♥ 1 tablespoon dried oregano
- ♥ dash salt
- ♥ dash pepper

Cut a thin slice off the top of each tomato.

Scoop out and discard pulp.

Invert tomato on paper towel to drain.

Combine cheese and onion.

Spoon into tomatoes.

In a jar combine oil, vinegar, oregano, salt, and pepper and shake well.

Spoon over tomatoes.

Cover and refrigerate for 30 minutes.

Mind Snacks!

- ♥ It's a sure thing you won't finish if you don't start.

- ♥ The average pencil is seven inches long, with just a half-inch eraser - in case you thought optimism was dead.

Stuffed Mushrooms

Good by itself, but also makes a nice garnish.

- ♥ Box or two of large whole mushrooms
- ♥ 8 ounces of cream cheese
- ♥ dash tobasco
- ♥ dash A1 sauce
- ♥ dash salt
- ♥ dash mayonnaise
- ♥ dash Worcestershire sauce

All the dashes depends on how much you want for taste. Experiment.

Remove stems from fresh mushrooms.

Wash and allow to dry.

Stuff the caps with the mixture.

Sprinkle with paprika and serve.

Mind Snacks!

- ♥ The object of most prayers is to wrangle an advance on good intentions.

- ♥ Start each day with a smile and get it over with.

- ♥ Most of us can forgive and forget; We just don't want the other person to forget we forgave.

- ♥ Satisfaction: If you don't get everything you want, think of things you don't get that you don't want.

Taco Dip

Fit for a Mexican Fiesta!

- ♥ 1 - 8 ounce cream cheese (softened)
- ♥ 1 - 8 ounce package sour cream
- ♥ 1 package Taco seasoning
- ♥ 1 head of lettuce (chopped)
- ♥ 1 tomato (diced)
- ♥ ¾ cup grated cheddar cheese

Mix cream cheese and sour cream until smooth.

Stir in taco sauce until well mixed.

In glass pie plate spread lettuce on bottom then add sour cream mixture.

Sprinkle cheese and tomato on top.

Serve with Tostitos.

Mind Snacks!

- ♥ A friend that is not loyal is worse than an enemy.
- ♥ To have a right to do a thing is not at all the same as to be right in doing it.
- ♥ Always put off until tomorrow what you shouldn't do at all.

Beverages

Cocoa Mix

Nothing beats Cocoa for taking the chill out of the bones.

- ♥ 1 pound Nestles Quick
- ♥ 1 cup powdered sugar
- ♥ 1 jar (7 oz.) non-dairy creamer
- ♥ 1 pkg. (1 pound 9 ounce) dried milk

Mix together in large bowl.

Store in airtight jar.

To serve, mix 1/3 cup mixture with 1 cup very hot water.

Mind Snacks!

- ♥ Happiness is between too little and too much.
- ♥ You don't get harmony when everybody sings the same note.
- ♥ Don't expect anything original from an echo.
- ♥ Some people march to a different drummer - and some people polka.

A Dream Come True!

When we lived in Mission Viejo, I played golf every week with the ladies group. Also on Friday there were twelve of us that would go out early and play the back nine before the men were ready for the back nine. Then we would go in and have breakfast together.

One night I dreamed I had a hole-in-one on the back nine but the Pro said it would not count because I had to play the front nine and since it was busy with men I couldn't play it. I told everyone at our breakfast about my dream. Since I'm not one of the world's best golfers, it was particularly funny.

Exactly two weeks later, we were playing the seventeenth hole when I took my seven wood and hit a shot straight to the green and it just rolled in. There was a man raking the sand trap and he didn't know what to do so he got on his cart and came back and hugged me.

By the time we got to the clubhouse everyone knew about it. Unlike my dream the Pro said, "You have to play the front nine for this to count. Anytime your group is ready let me know because none of the men will mind you cutting in!" I told the Pro that I had to get something to eat and call my husband and we would be ready within the hour.

I called my husband at work and his secretary said, "Peggy, he's in a very important meeting and asked not to be disturbed." I said, "Mary, disturb him, I want every man in that room to know what I have just done."

We played the front nine and my score was horrible. Every now and then as I went to take a shot some man would run up and hug me. I often wondered what "Headquarters" said when they received my score card. How could someone play so badly on the front nine and have a hole-in-one on the back nine.

Cranberry Punch

Tart but delicious:

- ♥ 1 pound can jellied cranberry sauce
- ♥ ¾ cup orange juice
- ♥ ¼ cup lemon juice
- ♥ 3 ½ cups ginger ale, chilled

Beat cranberry sauce until smooth.

Stir in juices.

Add ginger ale.

Serve over ice.

Makes 12 to 15 four ounce servings.

Mind Snacks!

- ♥ Be slow to start a fire you can't put out.
- ♥ The difference between a hero and a coward is one step sideways.
- ♥ Its when you run away that you are most likely to stumble.
- ♥ The best way to avoid a car accident is to travel by bus.
- ♥ A week-end is the shortest distance between two Mondays and the longest distance between two paydays.

Cranberry-Raspberry Sipper

From granddaughter Tori.

- ♥ 2 cups cranberry juice cocktail (chilled)
- ♥ 1 cup frozen raspberries
- ♥ 1 cup ice cubes
- ♥ mint sprigs (optional)

Blend cranberry juice and raspberries until smooth.

Sieve mixture and return to blender. (Discard seeds)

Add ice cubes and blend again until smooth.

Garnish with mint sprig and serve. (Makes 5 servings.)

Mind Snacks!

- ♥ The way to overcome shyness is to become so wrapped up in something that you forget to be afraid.

- ♥ The heart is the toughest part of the body. Tenderness is in the hands.

- ♥ Courage is contagious. When a brave man takes a stand, the spines of others are stiffened.

  (Rev. Billy Graham)

- ♥ You cannot do a kindness too soon, for you never know how soon it will be too late. *(Ralph Waldo Emerson)*

- ♥ Kindness is a language which the deaf can hear and the blind can read. *(Mark twain)*

Fruit Punch

A good party punch.

- ♥ 1 - 6 oz frozen orange juice
- ♥ 1 - 6 oz frozen lemonade
- ♥ 1 quart apple juice
- ♥ 2 quarts ginger ale

Mix together.

Pour over 1 quart of your favorite sherbet in a punch bowl.

Mind Snacks!

- ♥ No road is right if you have no destination.

- ♥ Gossip is that which no ones claims to like - but everybody enjoys.

- ♥ Flattery is alright - if you don't inhale. *(Adlai E Stevenson)*

- ♥ Those who bring sunshine to the lives of others cannot keep it from themselves.

- ♥ Gratitude is the memory of the heart.

- ♥ The hardest arithmetic to master is that which enables us to count our blessings.

- ♥ Go the extra mile. It's never crowded.

Peach & Melon Cooler

From granddaughter Tori.

- ♥ 1 cup fresh peaches
- ♥ 1 cup cantaloupe (cubed)
- ♥ 1 can lemon-lime soda (cold)
- ♥ 3 large strawberries

Blend peaches, cantaloupe, and a little lemon-lime soda until smooth.

Stir in remaining lemon-lime soda.

Serve over ice in tall glasses using the strawberries as a garnish.

(Makes three glasses.)

Mind Snacks!

- ♥ Fall seven times, get up eight. *(Japanese Proverb)*

- ♥ If you can find a path with no obstacles, it probably doesn't go anywhere.

- ♥ Only a fool argues with a skunk, a mule or the cook.

- ♥ Only a fool tests the depth of the water with both feet.

  (African Proverb)

- ♥ A fanatic is someone who can't change his mind and won't change the subject. (*Winston Churchhill*)

Shopping Abroad

In 1961 we moved from Bradenton, Florida to Rome, Georgia. Carol was starting first grade in Rome. The first day of school she wore a very cute dress (They wore dresses in those days.)

It was pale yellow with little people around the hem. Sounds awful but it was a cute dress. Her teacher said, "Carol, that is an unusually pretty dress. Where did your mother buy it".

Carol responded without hesitation and a demure smile, "She bought it abroad"!

Her teacher questioned her, "Do your parents go over seas often"? Carol confirmed that indeed her parents were often abroad.

I found out about this at the next parent-teacher meeting. I was surprised and shocked! We had never been overseas at that time.

Her teacher thought it was so cute she had told this story.

I did not share her opinon, and little Carol and I had a chat about "Shopping Abroad".

Mind Snacks!
♥ Don't approach a goat from the front, a horse from the back or a fool from any side. (*Yiddish Proverb*)
♥ Things are moving too fast when we are told we can microwave minute rice!

Grape Ice Tea

This is surprisingly good. A special treat! Or change the flavor to strawberry or other delightful tastes. Be adventurous.

- ♥ 9 cups water
- ♥ 9 lemon flavored tea bags
- ♥ 1 1/8 cups Welch's purple grape juice (not concentrated)
- ♥ Mint leaves
- ♥ Lemon slices

Bring water to a boil.

Steep tea bags in boiling water for 5 minutes.

Remove tea bags.

Stir in grape juice.

Chill.

Server over ice with a mint leaf and lemon slice.

Mind Snacks!

- ♥ When you make your mark on the world watch out for erasers.
- ♥ When there is a lot of it around, you never want it very much.
- ♥ Laziness is nothing more than resting before you get tired.
- ♥ Don't tell me how hard you work. Tell me how much you get done.
- ♥ Only God is in a position to look down on anyone.

Russian Tea

Also good on a cold night.

Actually, I keep this made up in a jar at all times.

You never know when you will want a cup of spiced tea!

- ♥ 2 cups Tang (orange drink)
- ♥ 1 ½ cup sugar
- ♥ 1 cup instant tea
- ♥ 4 scoops lemonade mix
- ♥ ½ tsp. cloves
- ♥ 1 tsp. cinnamon

Mix together and store in air tight jars.

To serve: Add 2 tsp. to a cup of hot water.

Mind Snacks!

- ♥ Take time:

  Take time to pray, it is the source of power!

  Take time to play, it is the source of perpetual youth!

  Take time to read, it is the fountain of wisdom!

  Take time to love, it is a God given privilege!

  Take time to be friendly, it is the road to happiness!

  Take time to laugh, it is the music of the soul!

  Take time to give, it is too short a day to be selfish!

  Take time to work, it is the praise of success!

Quick Punch

Very quick and smooth!

- ♥ 1 quart sherbet (your choice flavor)
- ♥ 3 - 12 oz bottles of lemon-lime carbonated beverage

Scoop sherbet into punch bowl.

Carefully add the 3 bottles of lemon-lime (lots of fizz!).

Stir gently.

Makes 25 to 30 four ounce servings.

Mind Snacks!

- ♥ Spite is never lonely; envy always tags along.

- ♥ Sometimes the best way to convince someone he is wrong is to let him have his own way.

- ♥ Love looks through a telescope; envy, through a microscope.

- ♥ The chains of habit are generally too small to be felt until they are too strong to be broken.

- ♥ A bad habit never disappears miraculously; it's an undo-it-yourself project.

- ♥ Attitude is the Mother of Luck.

- ♥ Our faults irritate us most when we see them in others.

Why Me and Not Mitch!

When we lived in Owensboro, Kentucky, Vic's parents came to visit. Our granddaughter Tori was three years old at that time. Tori is short for Victoria and belongs to my daughter Donna.

Great grandmother "Maime" wanted to go shopping and take little Tori with her. She wanted to buy her a cute dress. Our son Mitch, who was 10 at the time also insisted on going along and off they went!

Tori was not much focused on the shopping, but after Mitch got a new pair of jeans and a shirt, her interest grew. She insisted on blue jeans also, but Maime wanted her to have a nice dress.

Tori looked up at Maime with big eyes and pointed out, "You didn't make Mitch wear a dress!" She got her blue jeans.

During the visit, every time we left the house someone would remind little Tori to visit the bathroom. She finally asserted, "You don't make Mitch go to the bathroom, why do you tell me to go?" Obviously we had a trend developing and some things are just not easy to explain to a three-year-old.

Mind Snacks!

♥ None are so empty as those who are full of themselves.

♥ If you are wrapped up in yourself, you are overdressed.

♥ It is far more impressive when others discover your good qualities without your help.

♥ The egotist always hurts the one he loves - himself.

Breads, Muffins, Pancakes

Banana Bread

This takes a little time but it is worth every minute of it!

- ½ cup butter
- 1 cup sugar
- 2 eggs
- 1 ½ cups mashed bananas
- 1 tablespoon lemon or lime juice
- 2 cups flour
- 1 teaspoon soda
- ½ teaspoon salt
- ½ teaspoon cinnamon
- ½ cup chopped nuts

Cream together butter & sugar until light and fluffy.

Beat in eggs, one at a time.

Stir in bananas and lemon juice.

Mix together flour, soda, salt, and cinnamon.

Blend into creamed mixture.

Stir in nuts.

Bake in greased and floured pan at 350 degrees for 40 - 50 minutes.

(Substitute 2 cups shredded zucchini for bananas and you have great zucchini bread.)

Beer Muffins

Easy, good, and they make your kitchen smell great!

- ♥ 2 cups bisquick mix
- ♥ 1 tablespoon sugar
- ♥ 1 can warm beer

Mix together.

Pour in muffin tins. (fill half full)

Bake at 400 degrees until brown.

This will become a family favorite.

A Chip Off The Old Block

Because the kids ate free on Wednesday night at "Texas Lucy's", we often stopped there and ate before an Angel's baseball game. The waitresses were dressed very sexily. One night Victor IV, age 5, said "Granddad, do you think these girls are sexy?"

Vic said yes he did. Little Victor IV said, "Would you like to take one home with you?" Vic's answer, "Yes, but I don't think Grandmom would let me."

Cranberry Bread

Wow! Real pizzazz!

- ♥ 1 cup ground cranberries
- ♥ 1 cup sugar
  Mix together, let stand while mixing the following.
- ♥ 1 cup sugar
- ♥ 2 tablespoons of butter
- ♥ 1 egg
- ♥ 3 cups flour
- ♥ 4 teaspoons baking powder
- ♥ 1 teaspoon salt
- ♥ 1 cup milk
- ♥ ½ cup chopped pecans
- ♥ grated orange rind

Add the 2 mixtures together.

Bake 350 degrees for 1 hour in bread pan.

Mind Snacks!

- ♥ Of life's two certainties, death and taxes, only taxes is the one for which you can get an automatic extension.

- ♥ Everything comes to he who hustles while he waits.
  (Thomas a Edison)

- ♥ Dig the well before you are thirsty. *(Chinese Proverb)*

French Pancakes

I didn't know what section to put these in. A great breakfast for company!

- ♥ ½ cup flour
- ♥ ½ cup milk
- ♥ 2 eggs
- ♥ 6 tablespoons butter
- ♥ 1 bag of powdered sugar (16 ozs)
- ♥ 3 tablespoons lemon juice
- ♥ nutmeg

Combine flour, milk, and eggs. Beat with a wire whisk until lumpy.

In a 9x13 inch glass pan melt the butter.

Pour in egg, flour, milk mixture.

Bake 10 minutes at 425 degrees.

Sprinkle with powdered sugar.

Sprinkle with lemon juice.

Sprinkle with a little nutmeg.

Return to oven for 1 minute.

Cut out of pan in squares.

Serve with maple syrup or preserves.

Mind Snacks!

- ♥ Nostalgia is the ability to remember yesterday's prices while forgetting yesterday's wages.

Kentucky Corn Bread

The Kentucky way!

- ♥ 1 cup self-rising corn meal
- ♥ dash salt
- ♥ 1 egg
- ♥ ¾ cup milk

Mix together. Coat pan with 2 teaspoons of cooking oil.

Bake 350 degrees for 30 minutes.

May be baked in a small skillet or muffin tins.

We like our corn bread crusty so I prefer a skillet.

Mind Snacks!

- ♥ If your ship doesn't come in swim out to it.

- ♥ Be bold in what you stand for and careful in what you fall for.

- ♥ Standing in the middle of the road is very dangerous; you get knocked down by traffic from both sides. (*Margaret Thatcher*)

- ♥ If the window of opportunity appears, don't pull down the shade.

- ♥ Progress always involves risks. You can't steal second base and keep your foot on first.

The Goodyear Blimp

In 1987 we had the pleasant and exciting opportunity of getting to go up in the Goodyear Blimp. The weekend before we were to take our ride we had two of our grandchildren with us, and we were explaining the blimp and that we were going to take a ride in it.

They had never seen a blimp up close and didn't really understand what it was. Little Victor was only 4 years old and Ashley was 10.

Vic said, "We will just take a drive over to Long Beach and maybe it will be there for you to see". We were in luck!

We got out of the car and walked up close to the tethered blimp. Vic explained everything to them and they were very excited that we were going to get to ride the blimp.

Victor was very quiet on the way home. Finally he said, "Granddad, Can I go with you on the ride"?

Vic replied, "Well, they only have 6 seats and they have already invited six people". Little Victor mulled that over quietly for a few minutes, then finally piped up, "But Granddad, you have a lap"!

We agreed that Granddad did indeed have a lap, so we asked, but they wouldn't let us take him.

Mind Snacks!
♥   One secret of life is to make stepping stones out of stumbling blocks.
♥   A ship in harbor is safe - but that is not what ships are for.

Low Fat Pumpkin Bread

Tasty but respects your waistline!

- ♥ 1 1/3 cups pitted prunes (8 ounces)
- ♥ 6 tablespoons water
- ♥ 1 cup packed brown sugar
- ♥ 1 cup granulated sugar
- ♥ egg substitute to equal 4 large eggs
- ♥ 1 cup pumpkin puree (8 ounces)
- ♥ 2 2/3 cups flour
- ♥ 2 teaspoons baking powder
- ♥ 1 teaspoon baking soda
- ♥ 1 teaspoon cinnamon
- ♥ ½ teaspoon salt
- ♥ ½ teaspoon cloves
- ♥ ¼ teaspoon ground ginger
- ♥ ¼ teaspoon nutmeg

Preheat oven to 350 degrees.

Combine prunes and water in food processor or blender.

Pulse on and off until prunes are finely chopped.

In mixer bowl blend prune mixture with sugars.

Beat in egg substitute and pumpkin.

In another bowl, combine remaining ingredients.

Add to mixer bowl and blend thoroughly.

Spray two 8 ½ by 4 ½ inch loaf pans with vegetable cooking spray.

Spoon bread mixture into pans equally.

Bake one hour (until toothpick inserted in center comes out clean.

Raisin Bran Muffins

You won't believe how good these are! And you can have them every day.

- ♥ 1 box Post Raisin Bran flakes (15 ounces)
- ♥ 2 cups sugar
- ♥ 5 cups flour
- ♥ 5 teaspoons soda
- ♥ 2 teaspoons salt
  Mix these ingredients together and set aside.
- ♥ Beat 4 eggs in blender
- ♥ Add 1 quart buttermilk
- ♥ Add 1 cup Mazola oil

Mix together with dry ingredients until moist throughout.

Store in refrigerator in plastic covered containers. Keeps up to six weeks.

Do not freeze.

To prepare: Bake 20 minutes at 375 degrees in muffin tins ¾ full.

Nuts or blueberries may be added when you bake.

Mind Snacks!

- ♥ A man begins cutting his wisdom teeth the first time he bites off more than he can chew.

Sour Cream Rolls

Your guests will think you have baked all day!

- ♥ 1 cup butter
- ♥ 8 ounces sour cream
- ♥ 2 cups self rising flour

Combine butter and sour cream until smooth.

Add flour.

Bake at 350 degrees for 25 minutes or until brown.

Makes 36 rolls.

Mind Snacks!

- ♥ Experience is what you get when you don't get what you want.

- ♥ He who hesitates is last.

- ♥ If you wait, all that happens is you get older.

- ♥ The greatest mistake you can make in life is continually to be fearing you will make one.

- ♥ Admit your errors before someone else exaggerates them.

Candy & Holiday Treats

Almond Caramels

Easy. The only trouble is in the wrapping!

- ♥ 1 cup sugar
- ♥ ½ cup brown sugar
- ♥ ½ cup light corn syrup
- ♥ 1 ½ cup half-half cream
- ♥ 4 tablespoons butter
  Combine ingredients and cook, stirring occasionally to form ball at 248 degrees on candy thermometer.
  Remove from heat and add:
- ♥ 1 teaspoon vanilla
- ♥ ½ cup slivered almonds

Spread bottom and sides of 9x5x3 loaf pan with cooking oil spray (Pam).

Pour mixture in pan and cool at room temperature.

Cut in small squares and wrap each one in saran wrap.

Store in covered tins.

Do not refrigerate.

Mind Snacks!
♥ Cooperation, Friendship, and Love. These can only be attained by giving them away.

Chocolate Dip

Use for chocolate dipping candies. Peanut Butter Balls, Bon Bons, Spiders, Pretzels, etc.

- ♥ 1 large package chocolate chips
- ♥ ¼ block paraffin

Melt slowly in top of double boiler.

Use round-headed tongs to dip candy.

Mind Snacks!

♥   If at first you do succeed - try to hide your astonishment.

♥   The reward for work well done is the opportunity to do more.

♥   It doesn't matter if you win or lose, until you lose.

♥   One measure of leadership is the caliber of the people who choose to follow you.

♥   Nothing is work unless you'd rather be doing something else.

A Late Arrival

When our fourth child, Mitchell, was born in November of 1964, he was a most welcome addition to our family. The other kids were 10, 12, and 14. He was like a living toy for them. I finally had to arrange a schedule of who got to give him his next bottle, bath, and put him to bed so they wouldn't argue.

We had a very difficult time having him, and both he and I stayed in the hospital for two weeks. On Saturday morning around 10 am we arrived home. Neighbors came in and everyone wanted to hold him. We had been given a brand new item on the baby market at that time, a baby-carrying seat.

We put him in it and passed him around. When our son Victor, got his turn, he eliminated the seat, looked us in the eye, and said, "I want to hold him, not some dumb seat".

The baby seat was never used again!

Mind Snacks!

♥ Thanks to the Interstate Highway System, it is now possible to travel across the country from coast to coast without seeing anything.

(Charles Kuralt)

♥ The average tourist wants to go to places where there are no tourists.

♥ Mincing your words makes it easier if you have to eat them later.

♥ Be careful of your thoughts, they may become words at any moment.

Chocolate Bon Bons

Your guests will not believe you made them!

- ♥ 2 boxes powdered sugar
- ♥ 1 stick butter
- ♥ 1 can condensed milk (Eagle Brand)
- ♥ 2 cups coconut
- ♥ 2 cups pecan pieces

Mix together and form into small balls.

Refrigerate for 1 hour.

Prepare chocolate dip mix (see recipe on page 62).

Dip in chocolate dip mix.

Store in tins in refrigerator.

Makes approximately 150 balls.

Karen and Sharks

When Karen was only three years old, the family came to visit us in California. We had a swimming pool in the back yard. Karen was not afraid of the devil himself, so we were constantly watching her. During the day she would jump into the pool at any time knowing someone would jump in after her.

At night we made Mitch, our teen-age son, sleep in the den so he could intercept her if she woke up and wanted to go swimming in the middle of the night.

Not until Karen was 22 years old did we know Mitch had told her that sharks always came in after dark when the lights were out. She said she knew we worried about her but she wasn't about to go swimming at night with the sharks.

Chocolate Fudge

The kids will really love this.

- ♥ 1 can small carnation milk
- ♥ 1 stick butter
- ♥ 1 cup nuts
- ♥ 1 teaspoon vanilla
- ♥ 3 packages chocolate chips
- ♥ 1 pint marshmallow creme

Cook sugar, milk, and butter together.

When it starts to boil, begin timing and boil for 10 minutes.

Remove from stove and add chips, marshmallow crème, and nuts.

Beat and pour quickly into a dish and let cool.

Mind Snacks!

- ♥ Nothing wilts faster than laurels that have been rested on.
- ♥ Blessed are they who have nothing to say and who cannot be persuaded to say it.

Church Windows

So easy and so good!

- ♥ 1 stick butter
- ♥ 12 oz. Package chocolate chips
  Melt together in top of double boiler. When melted remove from heat and add:
- ♥ 3 cups miniature marshmallows (colored ones if you can find them)
- ♥ 1 cup pecan pieces

Roll in 2 logs. Wrap in wax paper and chill.

Slice and serve.

Store in tins in refrigerator.

Mind Snacks!

♥ Have you noticed that these days even a moment of silence has to be accompanied by background music?

♥ A leading authority is anyone who has guessed right more than once.

♥ To disagree, one doesn't have to be disagreeable.

(Barry M Goldwater)

Crispy Chocolate Bars

Oh! If only chocolate wasn't so fattening!

- ♥ 1 cup chocolate chips
- ♥ 1 cup butterscotch chips
- ♥ ½ cup crunchy peanut butter
- ♥ 5 cups corn flakes

Combine chips and peanut butter in large saucepan.

Stir over low heat until smooth.

Add cereal.

Stir until well coated.

Spread mixture evenly into 9x9x2 pan.

Chill until firm.

Cut into squares.

Mind Snacks!

- ♥ Public opinion is like the castle ghost; no one has ever seen it, but everyone is scared of it.

- ♥ Advice is what we ask for when we already know the answer but wish we didn't.

Date Puffs

Simply delicious!

- ♥ 1 pound chopped dates
- ♥ ½ cup butter
- ♥ 1 ½ cup Rice Krispies
- ♥ 1 cup pecan pieces
- ♥ ½ cup sugar
- ♥ 1 teaspoon vanilla

Cook dates, butter, and sugar over low heat until smooth paste.

Remove from heat.

Add vanilla, Rice Krispies, and nuts.

Mix well and roll into small balls.

Roll balls in powdered sugar.

Store in tins in refrigerator.

Mind Snacks!

- ♥ Cooperation must start at the head of a department if it is expected at the other end.

- ♥ Prayer is when you talk to God; meditation is when you listen to God.

- ♥ What we usually pray to God is not that His will be done, but that He approve ours.

Divinity

This one is special. Not many people make good divinity.

- ♥ 2 ½ cups sugar
- ♥ ½ cup cold water
- ♥ ½ cup white Karo syrup
- ♥ ½ cup finely chopped pecans
- ♥ 2 egg whites
- ♥ 1 teaspoon vanilla

Combine sugar, water, and syrup.

Cook until it runs off spoon as fine hair.

Pour ½ the syrup mixture over 2 stiffly beaten egg whites.

Cook balance of the syrup mixture a minute longer and then pour in the egg mixture.

Beat until cool.

Add vanilla & nuts.

Spoon on wax paper and put a full half pecan on top of each.

Mind Snacks!

- ♥ Leave everything a little better than you found it.
- ♥ Call on God, but row away from the rocks.
- ♥ Education is learning what you didn't even know you didn't know.

Marvelous Macaroons

Simply marvelous!

- ♥ 2 2/3 cup coconut
- ♥ 2/3 cup sugar
- ♥ ¼ cup flour
- ♥ ¼ teaspoon salt
- ♥ 4 egg whites, beaten
- ♥ 1 teaspoon almond extract
- ♥ 1 cup chopped almonds

Combine first four ingredients.

Stir in egg whites and extract.

Stir in almonds.

Mix well.

Drop by teaspoon onto lightly greased baking sheet.

Garnish with cherry halves.

Bake at 325 degrees for 20-25 minutes. (Edges should be golden brown).

Remove from baking dish immediately.

Mind Snacks!

♥ The difference between reality and fiction? Fiction has to make sense.

Peanut Butter Balls

Has very broad appeal!

- ♥ 2 sticks butter, melted
- ♥ 1 cup crunchy peanut butter
- ♥ 1 box powdered sugar

Mix and refrigerate for 1 hour.

Roll into small balls and refrigerate for 1 hour.

Dip in chocolate (see recipe for chocolate dip).

Dad Backed Up and Hit Him Again

I was having my church group for dinner and Vic left to go pick up a girl who was going to help with the dishes and serving. He took Mitch with him (age 4). They didn't come back and I began to worry, especially since all the guests were arriving.

Finally here they came in a police car. Forty people were at the front door wondering what had happened. Mitch spoke first, "Mom, Dad hit a car and backed up and hit him again!"

Knowing everyone was all right, we all laughed with relief. Some guy ran a stop sign and Vic hit him and the impact threw Mitch against the dash which made him think Vic hit the car twice.

Thank goodness no one was hurt and Mitch didn't offer his explanation to the Police!

Our Own Ken Doll

When we brought little Mitchell home (my fourth child) we had a helper for a few weeks until I got completely back on my feet. Around noon one day, guest had just left, and I asked the helper to put him in bed for his nap.

About thirty minutes later more guests arrived to meet little Mitchell. Mary went to get him and returned quickly saying, "Mrs. Anderson, he's gone"! I sighed and replied, "Find the other three kids and you'll find him".

She returned saying, "I found Donna and Victor, but I didn't find Carol (or the baby). I replied, "Find her and you'll find him".

She went to the basement and there was Carol and her best friend Ginger trying outfits on the baby. He was only two weeks old!!

That was the way Mitchell grew up. He was picked up, put down, and played with constantly. He never cried for anything. He never had the opportunity! There was always someone catering to him.

He has grown up to be a fine young man!

Mind Snacks!

♥ Enjoy the little things, for one day you may look back and realize they were the big things.

♥ Country music is three chords and the truth.

♥ People who make music together cannot be enemies, at least not while the music lasts.

♥ Learning music by reading about it is like making love by mail.

Rice Krispies Bars

A favorite of the kids from 6-90!

- ¼ cup butter
- 4 cups miniature marshmallows
- 5 cups rice krispies

Melt butter.

Add marshmallows and stir until melted and well blended.

Remove from heat and add rice krispies.

Stir until well coated.

Press mixture evenly into greased 13x9x2 pan.

Cool completely before cutting.

Mind Snacks!

- All I have seen teaches me to trust the Creator for all I have not seen. (*Ralph Waldo Emerson*)

- If you are not as close to God as you used to be, who moved?

- Laughter is the shortest distance between two people.

- Success is getting what you want. Happiness is liking what you get.

- Probably nothing in the world arouses more false hope than the first hours of a diet.

Spiders

Another easy one that almost everyone loves.

- ♥ 2 - 6 ounce packages of chocolate chips
- ♥ 2 - 6 ounce packages of butterscotch chips
- ♥ 2 - 6 ounce cans of chowmein noodles
- ♥ 2 cups peanuts or cashews

Melt chips in top of double boiler.

When melted remove from heat and quickly stir in noodles and nuts.

Coat completely.

Drop by teaspoon onto wax paper.

Refrigerate then store in tins in refrigerator.

Hot Apple Pie

My son Victor and his family lived in San Dimas, California, near us. This was wonderful for me because I could see two of my grandchildren frequently.

I often picked up my grandson Victor IV at playschool and took him to McDonald's for lunch.

One day after we had eaten our Happy Meal, he said, "Grandmom, McDonald's have something new." "Oh, I said. What is it?" He said "Hot Apple Pie."

I said, "I guess you'd better have one." I went to counter, purchased one and brought it back to the table. He said, "Grandmom, do you want a bite?" I said that I did.

He said "Here, you take the first bite because it doesn't have as many apples in it!"

Swedish Nuts *

A must for every party.

Of all the things I have ever made, this is probably the #1 most asked for recipe.

My Aunt Clara gave me this many years ago.

And it is so easy to make!

- ♥ 2 egg whites, beaten stiff
  Add: dash salt
- ♥ Add 1 cup sugar

Fold in ¾ cup pecans or walnut halves

Melt ½ cup butter in a shallow pan.

Put nut mixture in pan and bake at 325 degrees for 30 minutes, turning every ten minutes.

Drain on paper towels.

Store in tins.

Will keep several weeks (if you hide them!!).

Mind Snacks!

- ♥ A swelled head doesn't always indicate a surplus of brains.

- ♥ If it weren't for the fact that the TV set and the refrigerator are so far apart, some people wouldn't get any exercise at all.

- ♥ Your body is the baggage you must carry through life. The more excess baggage, the shorter the trip.

Cakes

Better than Sex Cake!

Really? Well it depends, but it's pretty close!

- ♥ 1 box yellow cake mix
- ♥ 4 eggs
- ♥ 1 box instant vanilla pudding
- ♥ 1 - 8 ounce package of cream cheese
- ♥ 1 - 6 ounce package of chocolate chips
- ♥ 1 bar German Sweet Chocolate, grated
- ♥ ½ cup oil
- ♥ ½ cup water

Beat eggs.

Add the rest of the ingredients.

Bake at 350 degrees for 55 minutes in bundt pan.

Ice with German Chocolate Icing (see recipe on page 87).

Mind Snacks!

- ♥ Laurels don't make much of a cushion.

- ♥ So many people spent their health gaining wealth, and then have to spend their wealth to regain their health.

Carrot Cake

The best carrot cake we ever had!

- ♥ 1 ½ cup flour
- ♥ 1 teaspoon cinnamon
- ♥ ¾ cup sugar
- ♥ ½ teaspoon salt
- ♥ 1 teaspoon baking powder
- ♥ 2/3 cup oil
- ♥ 1 teaspoon soda
- ♥ 2 eggs
- ♥ 1 teaspoon vanilla
- ♥ 1 cup finely shredded carrots
- ♥ ½ cup crushed pineapple (drained)

Stir together all dry ingredients and add other ingredients.

Mix together until moist throughout and beat in electric mixer 2 minutes.

Pour into 9 x 9 x 2 pan.

Bake at 350 degrees for 35 minutes and let cool.

For Frosting, cream together:

- ♥ 1 - 3 ounce cream cheese
- ♥ 4 tablespoons butter,
- ♥ 1 teaspoon vanilla

Gradually add 2 ½ cups powdered sugar, blending well.

Put ½ cup pecan pieces on top.

77

Cherry Cheese Cake

My grandchildren's favorite!

- ♥ 1 - 9 inch graham cracker crust
- ♥ 1 - 8 ounce cream cheese
- ♥ 1 can condensed milk (Eagle brand)
- ♥ 1/3 cup lemon juice
- ♥ 1 teaspoon vanilla
- ♥ 1 can cherry pie filling

In large bowl, beat cheese until fluffy.

Gradually beat in condensed milk until smooth.

Stir in lemon juice and vanilla.

Pour into prepared crust.

Chill 3 hours.

Top with cherry pie filling.

A BLT Without the LT

One day my grandson, Victor IV, and I went out to lunch. I ordered a BLT.

He said that's what he wanted too but with out the lettuce and tomatoes!

Chess Cake

A southern favorite. The grandkids love this one.

- ♥ 1 box yellow butter cake mix
- ♥ 1 egg
- ♥ 1 stick butter, melted

Mix together and spread in 9 x 13 pan.

For second layer.

- ♥ 1 - 8 ounce cream cheese
- ♥ 2 eggs
- ♥ 1 box powdered sugar

Beat until creamy and spread over first layer.

Bake 350 degrees for 40 minutes.

Let cool and cut into squares.

Mind Snacks!

- ♥ Thinking is the hardest work there is, which is probably the reason so few engage in it.

- ♥ Keep your face to the sunshine and you cannot see the shadows.
  (Helen Keller)

- ♥ Nothing lasts forever - not even your troubles.

- ♥ Some people are always grumbling that roses have thorns; I am thankful that thorns have roses.

Chocolate Cake

Never fails, great tasting and moist.

- ♥ Devils food cake mix
- ♥ 1 pkg. Chocolate instant pudding
- ♥ 1 small sour cream
- ♥ ½ cup Wesson oil
- ♥ ½ cup warm water

Blend all ingredients.

Add:

- ♥ 4 eggs
- ♥ 1 large package chocolate chips

Pour into greased bundt pan.

Bake 60 minutes at 350 degrees.

Sprinkle with powdered sugar.

Mind Snacks!

- ♥ The best birthdays of all are those that haven't arrived yet.

- ♥ Storms make trees take deeper roots.

- ♥ Miracles sometimes occur, but one has to work terribly hard for them.

- ♥ It's hard to detect good luck - it looks so much like something you've earned.

Coconut Cake (Ugly Duckling)

Absolutely the best cake you ever ate and the easiest to make.

- ♥ 1 yellow butter cake mix

Cook as directed in loaf pan.

Mix together:

- ♥ 1 can eagle brand milk
- ♥ 1 can crème of coconut

Poke lots of holes in hot cake and pour mixture over cake.

Icing: When cake is completely cool, frost with following ingredients mixed together.

- ♥ 1 box (9 ounce) cool whip
- ♥ 1 cup coconut

Store in refrigerator.

Mind Snacks!

- ♥ Nothing is really lost, It's just where it doesn't belong.
- ♥ Some people suffer in silence louder than others.
- ♥ Showing up is 80 percent of life.
- ♥ The darkest hour has only 60 minutes.
- ♥ The way I see it, if you want the rainbow, you gotta put up with the rain. (*Dolly Parton*)

Chocolate Desert Cake

This one gets baked once a year, Vic's Birthday!!

- ♥ ¾ cup sugar
- ♥ 4 stiff beaten egg whites
- ♥ 4 well beaten egg yolks
- ♥ 6 tablespoons flour
- ♥ ½ teaspoon baking powder
- ♥ 2 ounces unsweetened chocolate
- ♥ 1 teaspoon vanilla
- ♥ ¾ cup flavored whipped cream
- ♥ Hungarian Chocolate Frosting (see recipe below)

Gradually mix sugar and egg whites.

Fold in the beaten egg yolks.

Add flour and baking powder.

Fold in melted unsweetened chocolate and vanilla.

Spread thinly in 11 x 16 inch cookie sheet lined with wax paper.

Bake in oven at 400 degrees for 15 minutes.

Turn out on cloth sprinkled with powdered sugar.

Trim edges, remove paper, and cool.

Cut into quarters (4 pieces).

Spread 3 of the quarters with the flavored whipped cream.

Stack the quarters with the quarter without whipped cream on top and match the edges.

Spread top and sides with Hungarian Chocolate Frosting.

(To make the Hungarian Chocolate Frosting: Melt 1 ounce of unsweetened chocolate and 1 ounce of sweet chocolate in top of double boiler. Add ½ cup powdered sugar sifted, 1 tablespoon hot water, and whole egg; beat; add 3 tablespoons margarine.)

Coconut Pound Cake

Great for morning coffees!

- ♥ 2 cups sugar
- ♥ 2 sticks butter
- ♥ 6 eggs
- ♥ 1 - 12 ounce package vanilla wafers, crushed
- ♥ 2 cans coconut
- ♥ 1 cup pecan pieces
- ♥ 1 teaspoon vanilla

Cream the butter and sugar.

Blend the eggs in one at a time.

Add wafers, nuts, coconut & vanilla.

Bake 325 degrees for 1 hour and 15 minutes in a bundt pan.

Mind Snacks!

- ♥ More things grow in the garden than the gardener sows.
  (Spanish Proverb)

- ♥ Striving for success without hard work is like trying to harvest where you haven't planted.

Dump Cake

How can anything be so easy and be so good!

Melt 2 sticks butter in loaf pan. 9" x 13"

Add:

- ♥ 1 can crushed pineapple
- ♥ 1 can cherry pie filling
- ♥ 1 box yellow cake mix (dry)

Add:

- ♥ 1 cup pecan pieces on top

Bake 350 degrees for 1 hour.

Mind Snacks!

- ♥ Everything looks impossible to the people who never try anything.

- ♥ Start by doing what's necessary, then what's possible and suddenly you are doing the impossible.

- ♥ Superstition is foolish, childish, primitive, and irrational - but how much does it cost you to knock on wood?

- ♥ Some people have all the luck. And they're the ones who never depend on it.

Fresh Peach Cake

Delicious! Worth the trouble.

Combine:

- ♥ 2 cups slice fresh peaches
- ♥ ¼ cup sugar
- ♥ ¼ cup orange juice

Set aside.

Combine to make cake batter:

- ♥ 1 package yellow cake mix
- ♥ 1 package instant vanilla pudding
- ♥ 1 cup water
- ♥ 4 eggs
- ♥ ¼ cup oil

Beat cake batter with mixer for 2 minutes.

Drain the peach slice mixture.

Pour ½ of cake batter into a greased 13x9x2 pan.

Arrange peach slices on top.

Cover with remaining cake batter.

Bake at 350 degrees for 40 minutes.

Let cool.

For Icing combine:

- ♥ 1 ½ cup slice peaches
- ♥ 1 tablespoon sugar
- ♥ 1 tablespoon orange juice

Set aside for 20 minutes.

Drain and mix with cool whip and frost the cake.

Justin Makes Soup!

(My daughter Donna shared with me the following story about my grandson Justin. I felt it was appropriate to include in my cookbook.)

One day Justin came into the living room and said, "I'm hungry. When do we eat?" It wasn't near dinnertime so I replied, "Dinner won't be for quite a while. Why don't you make a bowl of your favorite soup?"

Justin had never prepared soup before so I proceeded to give him instructions. "First place the soup in a large pan, add a cup or so of water or milk (he loves Clam Chowder), set the heat pretty low, watch it carefully, when it begins to boil stir it gently, then shut off the heat and carefully pour into a large bowl, get out the crackers and chow down!"

In a flash he was in the kitchen and I could hear the preparations begin. I decided to leave him on his own but continued to listen carefully.

About 15 minutes later he came running back into the living room and asked how could he tell when the soup was boiling. I told him to watch carefully for little bubbles but not to get his face directly over the pan. Off he went again.

In a few minutes he was back and asked, "How could he see the bubbles?" I told him to look at the top of the soup and he would see little bubble form and pop. Off he went, but was soon back again.

He couldn't see any bubbles on the soup but he could in the water. Well this raised my eyebrows. How could he possibly be seeing the water boil separately from the soup?

Off I go into the kitchen with Justin and on the stove I see the pan placed accurately on the burner, which was set nice and low. But in the pan is an unopened can of soup with the water surrounding the can boiling nicely.

Needless to say I shut the burner under the soup off quickly and vacated the kitchen while the soup cooled.

So I learned two important lessons: You can boil a can soup for 5 minutes or so without it exploding (don't recommend you try this), and always be explicit when providing cooking instructions to a male of any age!

German Chocolate Icing

Use on the Better than Sex Cake or other cakes.

- ♥ 1 cup evaporated milk
- ♥ 1 cup sugar
- ♥ 3 slightly beaten egg yolks
- ♥ ½ cup butter
- ♥ 1 teaspoon vanilla
- ♥ 1 cup chopped pecans

Cook first 5 ingredients and stir over medium heat until thickened, about 12 minutes.

Add pecans (You may add 1 cup coconut also).

Cool until thick enough to spread, beating occasionally.

Mind Snacks!

- ♥ If a man had as many ideas during the day as he does when he has insomnia, he'd make a fortune.

- ♥ Riches are not from an abundance of worldly goods, but from a contented mind.

Hummingbird Cake

They'll all be humming when they eat this!

- ♥ 3 cups flour
- ♥ 2 cups sugar
- ♥ 1 teaspoon soda
- ♥ 1 teaspoon salt
- ♥ 1 teaspoon cinnamon
- ♥ 3 eggs well beaten
- ♥ 1 cup oil
- ♥ 1 ½ teaspoon vanilla
- ♥ 1 - 8 ounce can crushed pineapple
- ♥ 1 cup pecan pieces
- ♥ 2 cups mashed bananas

Combine first 5 ingredients.

Fold in eggs and oil until all ingredients are moist.

Do not beat.

Stir in vanilla, pineapple, pecans, and bananas.

Bake at 350 degrees for 30-40 minutes

Mind Snacks!

- ♥ There are two specific ways you can take the initiative for setting the wages you demand. 1) Adopt the principle of doing more than you are paid for or 2) have a specific goal in life aimed at achievement above the level of mediocrity.

Prune Cake

A famous Christmas cake in Kentucky!

Mix following ingredients in order:

- ♥ 3 eggs
- ♥ 2 cups sugar
- ♥ 1 cup vegetable oil
- ♥ 1 cup buttermilk
- ♥ 2 cups flour
- ♥ 1 cup diced prunes
- ♥ 1 cup pecan pieces
- ♥ 1 teaspoon soda
- ♥ 1 teaspoon cinnamon
- ♥ ½ teaspoon nutmeg
- ♥ ½ teaspoon salt
- ♥ 1 teaspoon all-spice

Bake at 350 degrees for 45 minutes in bundt pan.

Or 35 minutes in a loaf pan.

For Icing:

- ♥ ½ cup sugar
- ♥ ½ cup buttermilk
- ♥ ½ teaspoon soda
- ♥ 1 tablespoon white corn syrup
- ♥ 6 teaspoon butter

Boil. Icing is done when a drop of icing will form into a ball when dropped into cold water.

Pour over cake.

Strawberry Cake

Easy, good, and very pretty!

- ♥ 1 box white cake mix
- ♥ 1 box (3 ounces) strawberry Jell-O
- ♥ ½ cup vegetable oil
- ♥ 3 eggs
- ♥ ½ large box frozen sliced strawberries (thawed)

Mix white cake mix, Jell-O, with ½ cup hot water.

Add oil, eggs and sliced strawberries.

Bake as directed on cake mix box.

Icing:

- ♥ ½ large box frozen slice strawberries (thawed)
- ♥ 1 box of powdered sugar
- ♥ 1 stick of butter

Mix powered sugar & butter until creamy, then add strawberries.

Mind Snacks!

♥ You'll miss 100% of the shots you don't take.

♥ Beach watching is like poking through years of attic collections. It's surprising what you see in trunks.

♥ Take a lesson from a clock. It passes time by keeping its hands busy.

Cookies

Chocolate Chip Raisin Oatmeal Cookies

With all this in them, they have to be good!

- ♥ 1 cup butter
- ♥ ¾ cup brown sugar
- ♥ 2 eggs
- ♥ 1 teaspoon vanilla
- ♥ 1 ½ cup flour
- ♥ 1 teaspoon soda
- ♥ ½ teaspoon baking powder
- ♥ 2 cups uncooked oats
- ♥ 1 - 12 ounce package chocolate chips
- ♥ 1 cup pecan pieces
- ♥ ½ cup raisins

Cream butter and sugar.

Beat thoroughly.

Add eggs and vanilla.

Beat well.

Add flour, soda, baking powder, oats, nuts, chips, and raisins.

Mix.

Drop by teaspoon on ungreased cookie sheet.

Bake at 350 degrees for 8-10 minutes.

Do not overbake.

Mexican Wedding Cookies

Nothing too much Mexican about them. But are they good!

- ♥ ¾ cup butter
- ♥ 4 tablespoons sugar
- ♥ 2 cups flour
- ♥ 1 cup pecan pieces
- ♥ 2 teaspoons vanilla
- ♥ 1 tablespoon milk
- ♥ powdered sugar

Cream butter and sugar.

Work in flour and nuts.

Add milk drop by drop.

Add vanilla.

Chill for 1 hour.

Form mixture into balls.

Bake at 350 degrees for 18 minutes.

Remove when crisp and roll in powdered sugar.

Mind Snacks!

- ♥ You're never a loser until you quit trying.

- ♥ Whenever you see a successful business, someone made a courageous decision.

No Muss, No Fuss Cookies

Just like the name, quick and easy.

- ♥ 1 stick of butter
- ♥ 1 package chocolate chips
- ♥ 1 can coconut
- ♥ 1 cup pecan pieces
- ♥ 1 can Eagle brand condensed milk
- ♥ 8 single graham crackers

Melt butter in sheet cake pan.

Crush graham crackers and sprinkle over butter.

Sprinkle chocolate chips, coconut, and pecan pieces over butter cracker mixture.

Pour can of condensed milk over all.

Bake at 350 degrees for 25 minutes.

Cut while warm.

Mind Snacks!

- ♥ The only thing that ever sat its way to success was a hen.

- ♥ Success has a simple formula: do your best, and people may like it.

- ♥ There are no secrets to success. It is the result of preparation, hard work, learning from failure.

Peanut Butter Cookies

My son Mitch's all time favorite. I've made a million of them!

- ♥ Ritz crackers
- ♥ Chunky peanut butter
- ♥ Chocolate dip (see recipe on page 62)

Make peanut butter sandwiches with Ritz crackers.

Dip in chocolate and place on cookie sheet. (Waxed paper helps!)

Chill

Mind Snacks!

- ♥ I think God 's going to come down and pull civilization over for speeding.

- ♥ Parents usually know where a teenage son is. He's in the family car. But they don't know where the car is.

- ♥ Someday science may be able to explain why a child can't walk around a puddle.

- ♥ The first thing a child learns after he gets a drum is that he's never going to get another one.

- ♥ Insanity is hereditary, but you get it from your kids.

GOLD'nBAKED Hams

GOLD'nBAKED honey glazed hams are available from franchise stores in southern California.

Our family started these stores.

The hams are excellent.

For the nearest GOLD'nBAKED Ham store, Call (949) 837-1426.

You can also order through the mail.

SOUPS: For low fat and low cholesterol diets, we suggest boiling the ham bone first and let it sit in refrigerator until the fat floats to surface.

Skim fat off top before using broth.

Ham Mixed Bean Soup

- ♥ 1 "Bag of Beans" (soak overnight in cold water)
- ♥ 1 chopped onion
- ♥ 1 can tomatoes
- ♥ salt & pepper to taste
- ♥ 1 GOLD'NBAKED HAM "SOUP BONE"

Put all ingredients in crockpot and cover with water.

Simmer 5 hours on high setting, covered.

Will need to add water.

Serve with corn bread.

Ham-Cheese Ball

- ¾ lb. ground GOLD'NBAKED HAM
- 1 - 8 oz. pkg. softened cream cheese
- 1 tsp. Worcestershire sauce
- 1 cup finely shredded sharp cheese
- 1 tsp. minced onion
- 3 drops Tabasco sauce

Combine all ingredients.

Shape into balls and roll in finely chopped pecans.

Chill.

Serve with crackers.

Make extra balls and freeze.

Mind Snacks!

- To help your children turn out well, spend twice as much time with them and half as much money.
- Never open the refrigerator when you're bored.
- A good example is the best sermon.

Ham Pea or Lentil Soup

- ♥ 1 bag of split peas or lentils
- ♥ 1 lb. sliced carrots
- ♥ 1 large onion, chopped
- ♥ 1 cup celery, chopped
- ♥ salt & pepper to taste
- ♥ 1 ½ quart water
- ♥ 1 GOLD'NBAKED HAM "SOUP BONE"

Place all ingredients together in 5-quart crockpot.

Simmer all day on high setting.

Note: May need more water.

Mind Snacks!

♥ The harder you work, the luckier you are.

♥ Everybody wants to go back to nature - but not on foot.

♥ When I play with my cat, who knows if I am more of a pastime to her than she is to me.

Ham Breakfast Casserole

- ♥ 6 eggs
- ♥ 8 slices bread
- ♥ 8 slices velveta cheese
- ♥ 2 cups diced GOLD'NBAKED HAM
- ♥ 1 can cream of mushroom soup - add milk to make 3 cups
- ♥ 1 ½ tsp. mustard

Layer bread, cheese, ham.

Pour mixture of eggs, soup, milk over layers.

Let set overnight.

Bake at 325 degrees for 1 hour.

Sprinkle with Parmesan cheese.

Will serve 6 people.

For a luncheon casserole, add 1 10 ounce package of chopped broccoli.

Mind Snacks!

- ♥ If you want your children to improve, let them overhear the nice things you say about them to others.

Hearty Macaroni Salad

- ♥ 1 cup uncooked elbow macaroni
- ♥ ¾ lb. GOLD'NBAKED HAM, cut into strips
- ♥ 1 ½ cups diced sharp cheddar cheese
- ♥ 1 cup chopped celery
- ♥ ½ cup chopped onion
- ♥ 1 ½ cup chopped sweet pickle
- ♥ ½ cup commercial sour cream
- ♥ 2 tablespoons prepared mustard
- ♥ Celery leaves (optional)

Cook macaroni according to package and drain.

Rinse with cold water; drain well.

Combine macaroni and next 7 ingredients.

Toss gently.

Cover and chill.

Garnish with celery leaves.

Yield 6 servings.

Mind Snacks!

♥ Charm is a way of getting the answer "yes" without asking a clear question.

Ham Patties

- ♥ 1 lb. GOLD'NBAKED GROUND HAM
- ♥ 2 tsp. GOLD'NBAKED HONEY MUSTARD
- ♥ 2 tsp. finely chopped onions
- ♥ ¼ cup cracker crumbs
- ♥ 1 egg
- ♥ 2 tablespoons barbecue sauce (optional)

Mix together

Make thin round patties (makes 12)

Fry slowly in vegetable oil

Serve with dollop of sour cream for something different.

Mind Snacks!

♥   Every artist was first an amateur.

Ham Dinner Casserole

- ♥ ¾ cup light cream cheese
- ♥ ¾ cup 1% milk
- ♥ 1/3 cup GOLD'NBAKED HAM mustard
- ♥ 2 tablespoons grated Parmesan cheese
- ♥ 2 cups cooked fettucini pasta (4 oz. uncooked)
- ♥ 2 cups cubed GOLD'NBAKED HAM
- ♥ ½ cup chopped tomatoes
- ♥ ½ cup frozen peas, thawed
- ♥ 2 tablespoons minced parsley

In large saucepan combine cream cheese and milk;

Cook over low heat, stirring until smooth.

Stir in mustard and Parmesan cheese.

Do not boil.

Add remaining ingredients.

Cook over low heat, stirring, until mixture is heated through about 5 minutes.

Makes 4 servings.

Serve with green salad for delicious one-dish meal.

Mind Snacks!

- ♥ Praise can be your most valuable asset as long as you don't aim it at yourself.

Raisin Sauce

- ♥ 1 ½ CUPS firmly packed brown sugar
- ♥ 1 ½ tablespoons all-purpose flour
- ♥ 1 ½ teaspoons dry mustard
- ♥ 1 ½ cups water
- ♥ ½ cup golden raisins

Combine all ingredients, stir well.

Cook over low heat, stirring constantly until thick.

Serve warm over GOLD'NBAKED HAMS.

Yield 2-1/3 cups sauce.

Mind Snacks!

- ♥ You may have to fight a battle more than once to win it.
- ♥ You can't look at a sleeping cat and be tense.

Salad Croissants

- ♥ 1 pkg. refrigerated, crescent dinner rolls
- ♥ 1 tablespoon prepared mustard
- ♥ ½ lb. GOLD'NBAKED HAM SALAD (ground ham, mayonnaise, pickle relish)
- ♥ ¼ cup shredded Cheddar Cheese

Unroll dinner rolls; cut each one in half to form a small triangle.

Spread a little mustard on each triangle.

Place ½ teaspoon GOLD'NBAKED HAM SALAD and a small amount of cheese near the longest side of each triangle.

Roll it up.

Place, seam side down on ungreased baking sheet.

Bake at 375 degrees for 11 to 13 minutes until golden brown.

Yield 16 appetizer servings.

Mind Snacks!

People drink for joy and become miserable.

People drink for sociability and become argumentative.

People drink for sophistication and become obnoxious.

People drink to help us sleep and wake exhausted.

People drink for exhilaration and end up depressed.

People drink to gain confidence and become afraid.

People drink to make conversation and become incoherent.

People drink to diminish our problems and see them multiply.

Richard Blummer

Sleeping Policemen

When Vic & I went to Jamaica on business we took a cab from the airport to the hotel. We drove across quite a few speed bumps. The cab driver turned and commented that here the speed bumps were called "Sleeping Policemen".

One day after we returned from our trip I was driving with my 5 year old granddaughter Ashley and we went over a speed bump in a parking lot.

I told her that in Jamaica they called them "Sleeping Policemen". She quietly absorbed that information.

About a month later Ashley was with me when we drove over another speed bump. She looked at me and said, "Grandmom, you ran over another" Dead Policeman". I said, "No dear, those are "Sleeping Policemen". "She fired back, "Well if you don't stop running over them, they are sure going to be dead!.

Mind Snacks!

♥ Any time you think you have influence, try ordering around someone else's dog.

Meat Dishes

Meat Loaf

Sticks to your ribs!

- ♥ 1 pound ground beef
- ♥ 1 egg
- ♥ ¼ cup milk
- ♥ 5 crackers, crushed
- ♥ 1 teaspoon salt
- ♥ 1 teaspoon Worcestershire
- ♥ catsup

Mix ground beef, egg, milk and crackers.

Add salt, pepper, and Worcestershire.

Mix well together and mold meat in glass pan.

Top meat with catsup.

Surround meat in bowl with a small amount of water.

Bake at 350 degrees for about 1 hour.

Mind Snacks!

♥ If you don't think dogs can count, try putting three dog biscuits in your pocket and then giving him only two of them.

Swedish Meatballs

Great for parties.

- ♥ 1 pound ground beef
- ♥ 1 onion
- ♥ 2 eggs
- ♥ cracker meal

Brown beef.

Sauté onion.

Beat the eggs.

Mix together and form into balls.

Steam in double boiler for one hour.

Mind Snacks!

- ♥ He who builds to every man's advice will have a crooked house.

- ♥ The only thing worse than hearing the alarm clock in the morning is not hearing it.

Worcestershire Roast

A real family favorite. Great for French Dip sandwiches.

- ♥ Rolled rump roast
- ♥ 1 small bottle Worcestershire mixed with 1 cup of water

Brown rump roast.

Pour bottle of Worcestershire over roast.

Bake uncovered for 4 hours at 250 degrees.

Wrap roast in foil and refrigerate.

Put juice in jar and refrigerate.

Next Day, slice roast and remove fat from juice.

Pour over roast, heat and serve.

Makes excellent beef dip sandwiches.

I often fix 3 roasts at one time, cut into slices, package in groups of 10 slices, and freeze. Freeze juice in jars. Warm up whenever and enjoy!

Mind Snacks!

- ♥ Ability is what will get you to the top if the boss has no daughter.

- ♥ An accountant is a man hired to explain that you didn't make the money you did.

- ♥ An actor is a guy who takes a girl in his arms, looks tenderly into her eyes, and tells her how great he is.

Donna Dresses Up!

Our eldest daughter Donna tended to be a bit on the precocious side. For example; A new acquaintance once invited Vic and I to attend their bridge club. Vic and I love to play bridge.

On this occasion it wasn't possible for little Donna, who was 1 ½ years old at the time, to stay with a baby sitter or with family, so we took her along.

Shortly after we began playing, Donna started to show signs of restlessness, so I asked the hostess if I could put her down for a nap. Perhaps in their bedroom.

She hesitated then agreed. Donna went to sleep very easily. A bit too easily I thought. I quietly shut the door, so we wouldn't wake her up, and went back to the bridge game. As the evening wore on I went to the door several times and listened. Not a sound!

When our bridge game ended I went, with our hostess, to retrieve Donna.

When I opened the door, quite a scene was spread out before me. Donna had somehow, quietly, managed to empty every drawer and closet into piles on the floor, and proceeded to mix and match jewelry, clothing, and make up. What a mess!

We offered to clean it up, but after taking in the mess, our host said don't worry about it. We quietly collected Donna and made a quick exit. Donna as an adult remembers this well and assures us she had a wonderful time!!!

Mind Snacks!

♥ Adolescence is the awkward area in the life of a youngster. They're too old for an allowance and too young for a credit card.

One Dish Meals

Beef Casserole

Mmmm good!

- ♥ 1 ½ pound ground beef
- ♥ 1 cup diced onions
- ♥ 1 can whole kernel corn
- ♥ 1 can cream of chicken soup
- ♥ 1 can cream of mushroom soup
- ♥ 1 cup sour cream
- ♥ salt & pepper
- ♥ bread crumbs
- ♥ butter
- ♥ thin noodles

Brown beef and onions.

Drain corn.

Cook noodles (3 cups) and place in casserole dish.

Add beef, onions, corn.

Mix chicken soup, mushroom soup, sour cream, salt, and pepper and pour over beef, onion, corn mixture.

Sprinkle bread crumbs on top.

Pour melted butter over crumbs.

Bake for 30 minutes at 350 degrees.

Beans and Barbecue Pork

Feeding a crowd? A great idea.

- ♥ 8 cans great northern beans
- ♥ 2 green peppers chopped
- ♥ 3 cups tomato catsup
- ♥ 6 cups barbecue sauce
- ♥ 4 cups hot picadilly sauce
- ♥ 1 cup brown sugar
- ♥ 4 onions quartered
- ♥ 3 pounds sliced barbecue pork

Mix and cook 2 hours.

Mind Snacks!

- ♥ A boy becomes an adult three years before his parents think he does - and about two years after he thinks he does.

- ♥ When you're safe at home you wish you were having an adventure; when you're having an adventure you wish you were safe at home.

Chicken Chow Mein

If you like Chinese, you'll love this!

- ♥ 3 chicken breasts
- ♥ ½ cup diced celery
- ♥ ½ cup diced green peppers
- ♥ 2 tablespoons soy sauce
- ♥ 2 tablespoons cornstarch
- ♥ ¼ cup cold water
- ♥ 2 cups chicken broth
- ♥ 3 ounces of drained mushrooms
- ♥ 5 ounces of water chestnuts, sliced and drained
- ♥ ½ pound of bean sprouts

Cook and dice the chicken breasts.

Cook the diced celery and green peppers until tender.

Mix the soy sauce, cornstarch, and cold water.

Add chicken broth to soy sauce, cornstarch, water mixture and cook until thick.

Add diced chicken, celery, and green peppers.

Add mushrooms, water chestnuts, and bean sprouts.

Heat and serve over rice or chow mein noodles.

Mind Snacks!

♥ Advice when most needed is least heeded.

Chicken Noodle Bake

Easy and good!

- ♥ 3 chicken breasts
- ♥ 2 cups noodles
- ♥ 1 can cream of mushroom soup
- ♥ 1 can of chicken broth

Cook and dice chicken breast.

Cook and drain noodles.

Mix mushroom soup and chicken broth and heat.

Add chicken to soup mixture.

Add noodles.

Mind Snacks!

- ♥ Old age is when you find yourself using one bend-over to pick up two things.

- ♥ By the time we learn to watch our step, we're not stepping out very much.

- ♥ No one is so old as to think he cannot live one more year.

- ♥ The woman who tells her age is either too young to have anything to lose or too old to have anything to gain. (*Chinese Proverb*)

- ♥ A person is always startled when he hears himself seriously called an old man for the first time.

Chicken Vegetable Casserole

A great one dish meal!

- ♥ 1 can cream of potato soup
- ♥ 1 cup milk
- ♥ salt
- ♥ 2 cups diced cooked chicken breast
- ♥ 1 bag frozen mixed vegetables (thaw & drain)
  Mix above together in 8x12 corning ware dish.
  Bake at 375 degrees for 20 minutes.
- ♥ ½ cup shredded cheese
- ♥ ½ cup french fried onion rings
- ♥ crescent rolls dough

Cut crescent roll dough in strips and lattice on top of casserole.

Bake uncovered 15 minutes longer.

Next top with cheese and french fried onion rings.

Bake uncovered 3 to 5 minutes longer.

Mind Snacks!

♥ The air is about the only remaining thing that's free, and it is becoming dangerous to breathe.

Easy Cheese Soufflé

Everyone will be impressed with this! A great addition for left over turkey dinners.

- ♥ Bread cubes
- ♥ 1 stick butter
- ♥ 3 eggs
- ♥ ½ teaspoon salt
- ♥ ½ teaspoon dry mustard
- ♥ ¼ teaspoon Tabasco sauce
- ♥ 2 cups milk
- ♥ 10 ounces grated cracker barrel cheese

Melt butter and toss together with bread cubes.

Separate the three eggs.

Beat egg yolks and add salt, dry mustard, Tabasco, and milk.

Add mixture to bread crumbs.

Add grated cheese.

Beat egg whites and fold in last.

Let set overnight.

Bake for 350 degrees for 45 minutes.

Mind Snacks!

- ♥ Some people have alarm clocks; I have my spouse's elbow.

My Son-In-Law the Movie Maker

In the late 1980's my daughter Donna and her family came, as usual, to spend Christmas with the family. Her husband Paul had a new toy; A video recorder. In those days they were huge clunky things that you had to place on your shoulder to use.

For the whole holiday, everywhere we went, Paul had this large camera on his shoulder making video. He recorded Christmas Tree Lane, the stars homes we drove them by, the Baskin-Robbins mansion lit up at night, and just about everything else he could.

On New Years eve, Vic decided to take a drive down Colorado Boulevard in Pasadena. This was especially exciting to our out-of-town family members who had heard lots of stories about how wild it gets there on New Years eve.

Paul positioned himself in the front passenger seat with his camera determined to get some video (for posterity). As they turned onto Colorado Boulevard Paul was frustrated trying to film out the passenger window. The camera was too big and there was always something on the other side of the street he wanted to tape.

My Vic, ever creative, opened the retractable sunroof in the van and suggested that Paul standup through the sunroof and film. Boy did this maneuver liven things up.

The people partying saw a man standing up chest high out of a van with a large official looking camera on his shoulder and assumed they were going to be on TV. Soon everyone was clowning to the camera.

Marshmallows flew at the VAN, canned string confetti shot every which way, and one girl even threatened Paul with an egg. When she threw it he caught it and it was hard-boiled!

Boy, did Paul get some fascinating footage. But when two girls threatened to "Moon" them they decide to retract Paul and the camera and calm things down. What a night!

115

Hot Chicken Salad

Good for luncheons.

- ♥ 2 cups chicken breasts, cooked & diced
- ♥ 2 cups celery
- ♥ ½ cup slivered almonds
- ♥ 1 cup mayonnaise
- ♥ 2 tablespoons lemon juice
- ♥ ½ teaspoon salt
- ♥ 2 teaspoons grated onion
- ♥ ½ cup grated cheddar cheese
- ♥ 1 cup crushed potato chips

Place the chicken breasts in a baking dish.

Layer the remaining ingredients in the sequence listed above (celery, almonds, mayonnaise & lemon juice, salt, grated onions, cheddar cheese, potato chips).

Bake at 350 degrees for 20 minutes.

Mind Snacks!

- ♥ Better to be alone than in bad company.

- ♥ Ambition may be all right, but it sure can get a fellow into a lot of hard work.

Lasagna

The very best!

- ♥ 2 eggs
- ♥ 3 pounds ground beef
- ♥ 3 small onions - diced
- ♥ 2 large cans tomato puree
- ♥ 2 large cans water
- ♥ 1 big can tomatoes - cut up
- ♥ salt & pepper
- ♥ 2 pounds Ricotta cheese (or cottage cheese)
- ♥ 3 pounds Mozzarella cheese
- ♥ Lasagna noodles

Brown ground beef.

Add onions, tomato puree, 2 cans water, cut up tomatoes, salt and pepper & stir.

Cook for mixture for 1 hour. (This makes your meat sauce.)

Beat 2 eggs and combine with Ricotta cheese or cottage cheese.

Grate the Mozzarella cheese.

Cook Lasagna noodles according to package instructions and rinse.

Combine ingredients as follows in large dish:

Noodles & Meat sauce (layer)

Noodles & Ricotta mixture (layer)

Mozzarella cheese & Meat sauce (layer)

Noodles & Meat sauce (layer)

Noodles & Ricotta mixture (layer)

Mozzarella cheese & Meat sauce (layer)

Bake 45 minutes covered at 350 degrees.

Peggy's Quick Goulash

- ♥ ½ pound ground beef
- ♥ 1 diced onion
- ♥ 2 cups uncooked macaroni
- ♥ 1 large can diced tomatoes
- ♥ salt and pepper

Brown ground beef with onions.

Add macaroni and tomatoes.

Salt and pepper to taste.

Cook until done.

Easy! Add a salad and French bread. A family favorite.

Mind Snacks!

- ♥ When arguing with a stupid person, be sure he isn't doing the same thing.

Spaghetti & Meat Sauce

Everyone says this is the best!

- ♥ 2 Tablespoons salad oil
- ♥ 1 ½ pound ground beef
- ♥ 1 large onion, diced
- ♥ 1 garlic clove, diced
- ♥ 2 teaspoons salt
- ♥ 6 ounce can tomato paste
- ♥ small can mushrooms
- ♥ ¾ cup tomato juice
- ♥ 1 teaspoon chili powder
- ♥ 1/8 teaspoon cayenne pepper

Brown ground beef and onions.

Add remaining ingredients and cook slowly for 1 hour.

Cook spaghetti as directed.

Rinse and serve with meat sauce.

Mind Snacks!

♥   Your children need your presence more than your presents.

♥ *Spicy Breakfast Casserole*

Great for a company breakfast. You can prepare it the night before.

- ♥ 1 pound bulk sausage
- ♥ 10 ounce package frozen artichoke hearts
- ♥ 8 eggs
- ♥ ¼ cup milk
- ♥ ½ cup black olives
- ♥ 1 cup mild chili pepper
- ♥ 1 cup grated jack cheese
- ♥ salt & pepper

Cook and crumble the sausage.

Steam artichoke hearts until tender.

Place sausage in 2-quart casserole.

Put artichoke hearts on top.

Combine 8 beaten eggs, ¼ cup of milk, and season with salt and pepper.

Pour over sausage and artichokes.

Sprinkle with ½ cup chopped olives, 1 cup mild chili peppers, and 1 cup grated cheese.

Bake uncovered at 325 degrees for 30 minutes.

Mind Snacks!

♥ There is nothing so annoying as arguing with somebody who knows what he is talking about.

Other Special Recipes

Acorn Squash

Delicious!

- ♥ Large acorn squash
- ♥ 2 tablespoons brown sugar
- ♥ 2 teaspoons butter
- ♥ cinnamon
- ♥ cheese strips

Cut squash in half (lengthwise).

Remove seeds.

Mix butter and brown sugar.

Fill each half of the squash with half of the butter brown sugar mixture.

Sprinkle with cinnamon.

Bake 1 hours at 300 degrees (uncovered)

Add sliced cheese strips on top in last 5 minutes of baking.

Mind Snacks!

♥ There are really only three types of people: those who make things happen, those who watch things happen, and those who say, What happened?

Banana Pudding

MMMMmmmmmmm!

- ♥ 2 cups vanilla wafer crumbs
- ♥ 2 sticks of butter
- ♥ 2 cups confectionery sugar
- ♥ 2 egg whites
- ♥ 3 or 4 sliced bananas
- ♥ 1 can crushed pineapple (drained)
- ♥ whipped cream
- ♥ chopped nuts (of your choice)

Spread vanilla wafer crumbs in medium baking dish.

Mix sugar, egg whites, and 2 sticks of melted butter and beat well.

Pour beaten mixture over vanilla wafer crumbs.

Spread sliced bananas on top.

Spread crushed pineapples over bananas.

Top with whipped cream and nuts.

Chill and serve.

Mind Snacks!

- ♥ On attitude: The world is full of cactus, but we don't have to sit on them.

Aunt Clara's Baked Pineapple *

This one has been incredibly popular. I get many requests for this! Great to take to a Pot Luck dinner!

- ♥ 2 16 oz cans chunk Pineapple drained
- ♥ 1 cup sugar
- ♥ 2 tablespoons flour
- ♥ 1 ½ cup grated cheddar cheese
- ♥ 1 cup crushed Ritz crackers
- ♥ 1 stick butter

Spread pineapple in medium greased baking dish.

Mix sugar and flour.

Cover pineapple with sugar and flour mixture.

Sprinkle with 1 cup of grated cheese.

Add Ritz crackers.

Melt butter and pour over top of everything.

Put additional ½ cup cheese on top.

Bake at 350 degrees for 40 minutes (uncovered).

Mind Snacks!

- ♥ Friendship: Never explain, your friends don't need it, and your enemies won't believe it anyway.

- ♥ Business: We are all manufacturers, some make food, others make trouble, and still others make excuses.

Baked Stuffed Tomatoes

Great as an extra for dinner!

- ♥ 6 eggs (hard boiled or fried)
- ♥ 4 slices bacon (fried and crumbled)
- ♥ 1 can whole corn (cooked and drained)
- ♥ 4 large or 6 medium tomatoes (whole)

Chop eggs and mix with bacon and corn.

Hollow out center of tomatoes. Wash and clean inside of tomatoes.

Stuff center of tomatoes with mixture.

Bake or microwave until heated thoroughly. (Don't over cook!)

They can also be served cold.

Mind Snacks!

- ♥ A baby boomer is a man who hires someone to cut the grass so he can play golf for the exercise.

- ♥ The back fence is the shortest distance between two gossips.

- ♥ The big advantage of being bald is that you can style your hair with a damp cloth.

Bread & Butter Pickles

Pickles never tasted so good!

- ♥ 4 quarts sliced cucumbers
- ♥ 3 cups sugar
- ♥ 3 red peppers cut into strips
- ♥ 3 green peppers cut in strips
- ♥ 1 quart vinegar
- ♥ 2 table spoons salt
- ♥ 4 onions cut into strips
- ♥ 4 tablespoons celery seeds
- ♥ 1 teaspoon dry mustard
- ♥ 1 teaspoon turmeric
- ♥ pinch alum

Mix together and boil 5 minutes. Makes 9 quarts.

Mind Snacks!

♥   Today a bargain is anything that is only moderately overpriced.

♥   Many a man goes into a bar for an eye-opener and comes out blind.

Victors Pie

Sometime in 1956…

A treat for "Mom" was to go out to eat after church every Sunday. We usually went to this little café that served "plate lunches" for $1.25. The food was all home made by a wonderful lady named Betty.

After lunch one Sunday, my oldest son Victor, who was three years old at the time, wanted a piece of chocolate pie. He wanted it very badly, but we rarely ordered dessert. However, on this day a big tear appeared in his eye, as he looked up at my husband Vic. In a choked voice he said, "But Daddy, I want it so bad". Well that was it. Vic gave in and ordered him a piece of the chocolate pie.

Little Victor was so excited he sat with his fork ready and when the pie arrived, he dove in. He gobbled the first bite and said, "I love chocolate pie". He ate another bite and said, "I like chocolate pie". Much more slowly he ate a third bite, looked up at us with a strange look on face, with his mouth slightly open, and muttered, "I don't like this chocolate pie".

His father tried a taste of the pie and discovered that the pie had been made with no sugar! Little Victor had been so excited to get his pie that it took him three bites before he realized it tasted bad!

Poor Betty, who had made the pie, was so embarrassed that she gave us our lunch free. (That rarely happens these days when restaurants make mistakes.) After that little Victor was prone to performing a little taste test before he gobbled his pie.

Cheese Sauce

A standard topping! Good over lots of different vegetables.

- ♥ 2 cups milk
- ♥ 2 tablespoons flour
- ♥ 2 tablespoons butter
- ♥ 2 cups shredded cheese
- ♥ 1 teaspoon Worcestershire

Mix milk, flour, butter, and cheese.

Cook until thick.

Add Worcestershire.

(For white sauce omit cheese.)

Mind Snacks!

♥ The most frightening horror tales are those told by the bathroom scales.

♥ Everything is difficult at first. (*Chinese Proverb*)

♥ Better to wear out than to rust out.

Eggplant Casserole

If you like eggplant, don't miss this one.

- ♥ 1 large egg plant (diced)
- ♥ 1 cup celery (diced)
- ♥ 2 tablespoons butter
- ♥ 3 pieces of crumbled toast
- ♥ 2 to 4 slices of bacon (fried & crumbled)
- ♥ Swiss cheese cut into thin strips

Boil eggplant and celery until tender.

Drain eggplant and celery and place in greased casserole dish.

Add butter and pieces of crumbled toast and mix together.

Sprinkle with bacon crumbles.

Place cheese strips on top.

Bake 350 degrees for 20 minutes.

Mind Snacks!

- ♥ If I can't be thin, please make all my friends fat.

- ♥ Middle age is when your narrow waist and broad mind exchange places.

- ♥ After looking at the bill for my operation, I understand why doctors wear masks in the operating room.

Grits Soufflé

You don't have to be southern to like this!

- ♥ 1 ½ cup regular grits
- ♥ 6 cups water
- ♥ 2 teaspoons seasoned salt
- ♥ 1 teaspoon onion salt
- ♥ ¾ teaspoon garlic salt
- ♥ ¾ teaspoon Worcestershire sauce
- ♥ ½ cup oleo, margarine, or butter
- ♥ 3 eggs (slightly beaten)
- ♥ 1 pound longhorn cheese (cubed)
- ♥ paprika

Cook the grits in 6 cups of boiling water for 5 minutes.

Stir in salts, Worcestershire sauce, and oleo.

Stir 2 to 3 tablespoons of the grits into the beaten eggs. Then stir the egg grits mixture into the grits.

Add cheese to the grits mixture. Stir until cheese melts.

Pour into 2 quart casserole dish.

Sprinkle heavily with paprika.

Cover and refrigerate over night.

Bake at 350 degrees for 1 to 1 ½ hours.

Serve hot!

Hot Potato Salad

A family favorite!

- ♥ 8 potatoes (cooked & diced)
- ♥ 1 cup mayonnaise
- ♥ 1 pound Velveeta cheese (diced)
- ♥ ½ cup chopped onion
- ♥ ½ cup sliced stuffed green olives
- ♥ ½ pound bacon (fried and crumbled)

Mix mayonnaise, cheese, onion, green olives, and bacon.

Add potatoes.

Place in greased casserole and bake at 350 degrees for 40 minutes (covered).

Mind Snacks!

- ♥ There are three ways to get something done:
  - Do it yourself
  - Hire someone
  - Forbid your children to do it
- ♥ A room without books is like a body without a soul. (*Cicero*)

Reunion Apples

Take to a family reunion or fix for a company outing or dinner. It's great!

- ♥ 8 cups cored and sliced cooking apples (about 9 small to medium apples)
- ♥ 1 cup sugar
- ♥ ½ teaspoon cinnamon
- ♥ ¼ teaspoon nutmeg
- ♥ ¼ cup oleo (margarine or butter)
- ♥ ¼ cup water

Place sliced apples in 13x9x2 (inch) dish.

In small bowl stir together sugar, cinnamon, and nutmeg.

Sprinkle this sugar mixture over the apples and stir together.

Place small dots of oleo on top.

Pour the ¼ cup of water over all.

Bake at 350 degrees for 40 minutes (covered)

Mind Snacks!

- ♥ Remember the good old days when a juvenile delinquent was a boy who played the saxophone too loud?

Sweet Potato Bake

Unbelievably good!

Main ingredients:

- ♥ 3 cups mashed sweet potatoes
- ♥ 3 well beaten eggs
- ♥ ¼ cup milk
- ♥ 1 teaspoon vanilla
- ♥ ½ cup melted butter
- ♥ 1 cup brown sugar

Topping ingredients:

- ♥ 1 cup brown sugar
- ♥ 1/3 cup flour
- ♥ 1 cup pecan pieces
- ♥ 1/3 cup butter (melted)

Mix together the main ingredients listed above and pour into a medium greased baking dish.

Mix together topping ingredients and sprinkle over the sweet potato main ingredients mixture.

Bake at 350 degrees for 30 minutes.

Mind Snacks!

- ♥ Many a man who misses an anniversary catches it later.
- ♥ One man's junk is another man's rare antique.

Pie and Cobblers

Cherry Cobbler

Grandmom's favorite.

- ♥ 1 cup flour
- ♥ 1 cup sugar
- ♥ 1 cup milk
- ♥ 1 stick butter
- ♥ 1 can cherry pie filling

Mix flour, sugar, and milk.

Melt butter in loaf pan.

Pour in mixture.

Add cherry pie filling.

Bake 350 degrees for 50 minutes.

Can substitute peach pie or other pie filling.

Mind Snacks!

♥ What counts is not necessarily the size of the dog in the fight - it's the size of the fight in the dog. (*Dwight D Eisenhower*)

♥ The biggest surprise the average husband can give his wife on their anniversary is to remember it.

Fresh Blackberry Cobbler

Granddad's favorite.

- ♥ 1 quart blackberries
- ♥ 3 cups sugar
- ♥ ½ quart water
- ♥ 8 inch uncooked pie crust
- ♥ 1 stick butter

Combine blackberries, sugar, and water. Heat mixture.

Pour over piecrust.

Add 1 stick of butter (cut up).

Add top crust.

Bake at 350 degrees for 45 minutes.

Mind Snacks!

♥ Before you drink at a brook, it is well to know its source.

♥ Adults are obsolete children. *(Dr. Seuss)*

♥ It takes about ten years to get used to how old you are.

♥ A budget is a system of reminding yourself that you can't afford the kind of living you've become accustomed to.

Meringue Pie Shells

They melt in your mouth.

- ♥ 6 egg whites
- ♥ 1 box powdered sugar
- ♥ 1 tablespoon cream of tartar
- ♥ pinch salt
- ♥ 1 tablespoon vanilla

Mix egg whites and powdered sugar and beat for 10 minutes on high speed.

Add cream of tartar and pinch of salt and beat for another 10 minutes on high.

Add 1 tablespoon vanilla to mix and spoon out onto cookie sheet lined with wax paper.

Press with spoon to form cup.

Bake 20 minutes at 250 degrees then 20 minutes at 275 degrees.

Fill with anything you like!

Mind Snacks!

- ♥ The longer the title, the less important the job.

- ♥ Invest in inflation. It's the only thing going up. (*Will Rogers*)

- ♥ Children need love, especially when they do not deserve it.

Southern Pecan Pie

Hard to beat when you want something sweet!

- ♥ 1 cup white Karo syrup
- ♥ ¾ cup sugar
- ♥ 3 large eggs
- ♥ 2 tablespoons butter
- ♥ 1 cup pecan pieces
- ♥ 2 tablespoon orange juice
- ♥ 8 inch unbaked pie shell

Beat eggs slightly.

Add sugar, juice, and syrup.

Stir in melted butter.

Spread pecans in pie shell.

Pour in filling.

Bake at 350 degrees for 50 minutes.

Mind Snacks!

♥ If you would like to buy an $18,000 car it's easy - buy a $ 6,000 car on time.

♥ The best security blanket a child can have is parents who respect each other.

Romantic Day

Every year Vic had a booth in a home show at Dodger Stadium. I would man the booth during the day and he and some of his salesmen would come in around four o'clock. On Friday, I had to man the booth and my grandson Victor IV, had the day off from kindergarten, so I asked him to come with me. I took coloring crayons, books, and toys to keep him entertained. That turned out to be unnecessary.

Across the aisle from our booth, a mother had taken her daughter for the same reasons. She and Victor IV became instant friends. I don't remember her name but we'll call her "Mary".

It started to rain in the middle of the day and a security man came by and asked the two kids if they would like to help carry some small animals inside under the tents in a make-shift area. They had a wonderful time carrying baby rabbits and other small animals. They thought they were so important because they were helping!

Later in the day there was an Elvis impersonator putting on a show. Mary and her mother invited Victor IV to go along with them. Naturally, I said yes.

Later Vic came in with another salesman and asked where Victor IV was. When I told him, he suggested we go and watch the show. When we arrived Elvis sang "Love Me Tender" and invited everyone to dance.

The only two people to come forward to dance were Victor IV and Mary. They held hands and swayed back and forth. It was so cute!

On our way home Vic and I were in the front seat and Victor IV was in the back in his car seat. Everyone was quiet. Finally, Victor IV said, "Granddad, I think this has been the most romantic day of my life!"

Strawberry Pie

Delicious!

- ♥ 1 cup sugar
- ♥ 1 cup water
- ♥ 3 tablespoons cornstarch
- ♥ 3 drops red food coloring
- ♥ sliced strawberries 1 quart or more
- ♥ 8 inch cooked pie crust

Mix sugar, water, cornstarch, and food coloring. Cook until thick.

Add sliced strawberries.

Pour into baked pie shell.

Mind Snacks!

- ♥ There are three periods in your life:

    - Youth

    - Middle Age

    - How well you look

- ♥ Learn to say "no"; it will be of more use to you than to be able to read Latin.

Salads

24 Hour Combination Salad

Great as a one dish luncheon!

- ♥ 1 head lettuce (shredded)
- ♥ ½ cup diced celery
- ♥ ½ cup diced green pepper
- ♥ 1 head cauliflower (cut up)
- ♥ 1 package frozen peas

Layer these ingredients. (Spread the lettuce in an appropriate container, then sprinkle celery, green peppers, cauliflower, and peas over the lettuce.)

- ♥ 2 cups mayonnaise
- ♥ 4 ounces grated cheddar cheese
- ♥ 2 tablespoons sugar
- ♥ 8 slices of bacon (fried & crumbled)

Mix this second group of ingredients and spread over layered salad ingredients.

Chill over night.

Toss well just before serving.

Mind Snacks!

♥ Character is much easier kept than recovered.

---

5 Cup Salad

So easy and good!

- ♥ 1 cup miniature marshmallows
- ♥ 1 cup pineapple chunks
- ♥ 1 cup mandarin oranges
- ♥ 1 cup coconut
- ♥ ½ cup sour cream

Mix and serve!

Mind Snacks!

- ♥ The hardest job kids face today is learning good manners without seeing any.

- ♥ It takes 17 muscles to frown and only 7 to smile.

- ♥ Feeling gratitude and not expressing it is like wrapping a gift and not giving it.

- ♥ The only part of the body that doesn't wear out with age is the tongue.

- ♥ Know yourself. Don't accept your dog's admiration as conclusive evidence that you are wonderful. (*Ann Landers*)

Apple / Grape Salad

A great salad to impress and please guests!

- ♥ 2 cups diced apples
- ♥ ½ cup seedless green grapes
- ♥ 8 marshmallows cut-up
- ♥ 2 cups chopped celery
- ♥ ½ cup pecan pieces
- ♥ ½ cup mayonnaise
- ♥ ½ cup cool whip or plain yogurt

Mix mayonnaise and cool whip (or yogurt).

Add other ingredients and chill.

Mind Snacks!

♥ If anything makes a child thirstier than going to bed, it's knowing that his parents have gone to bed too.

♥ Tomorrow is often the busiest day of the week.

♥ You cannot get ahead while you are getting even.

♥ Children have never been very good at listening to their elders, but they have never failed to imitate them.

Artichoke Salad with Vinaigrette Dressing

Something different. Very very good!

- ♥ 1 large package fresh mushrooms
- ♥ 1 can sliced black olives
- ♥ 3 cans artichoke hearts (drained & quartered)
- ♥ 3 fresh avocados, chopped
- ♥ Pimento (for color)

Toss together and serve with the following recipe for vinaigrette dressing.

- ♥ 4 tablespoons vinegar
- ♥ 2 tablespoons Dijon mustard
- ♥ 2 tablespoons chopped onion
- ♥ 4 tablespoons sugar
- ♥ 2/3 cup oil (of your choice)

Do not stir. Mix together by changing back on forth from one bowl to another.

You can put lemon juice on avocados and mushrooms to keep them from turning brown. They will last longer.

Mind Snacks!

- ♥ Childhood sometimes does pay a second visit to man; youth never.
- ♥ Remember that a successful marriage depends on two things:
    - Finding the right person
    - Being the right person

Cherry Bing Salad

A standard favorite.

- ♥ 1 can Bing cherries, pitted (save juice)
- ♥ 1 can crushed pineapple (save juice)
- ♥ 1 package cherry Jell-O (3 ounces)
- ♥ 1 package lemon Jell-O (3 ounces)

Heat juice from cherries and pineapple in place of hot water to dissolve Jell-O.

Mix cherries and pineapple and Jell-O mixtures in appropriate container and chill.

Mind Snacks!

- ♥ You can't say civilization isn't advancing; in every war, they kill you in a new way. (*Will Rogers*)

- ♥ Too hot to go to church? What about hell?

- ♥ Mrs. Casey Stengel on her marriage to Casey said; "For better or worse, but not for lunch!".

- ♥ Christmas is when you buy this year's gifts with next year's money.

Cranberry Jell-O Salad

This one is a lot of trouble, but worth it!

- ♥ 2 cups raw fresh cranberries
- ♥ 1 cup sugar
- ♥ 1 large package lemon Jell-O
- ♥ 2 cups hot water
- ♥ 1 cup pecan pieces
- ♥ 1 cup chopped celery
- ♥ 1 cup chopped apple
- ♥ 1 orange

Add sugar to cranberries.

Dissolve Jell-O with the 2 cups of hot water and pour mixture over cranberries.

Let mixture set until it begins to thicken.

Grind the orange and mix with pecan pieces, chopped celery, and chopped apple.

Add to Jell-O.

Chill and serve.

Mind Snacks!

- ♥ Common sense is not so common. (*French Proverb*)

- ♥ Man is very much like a bowl of apples. The apples that are seen on top are his reputation, but the apples down below represents his character.

Dump Salad

Easy to make and a favorite of our whole family.

- ♥ 1 3 ounce package of lemon Jell-O
- ♥ 1 3 ounce package of lime Jell-O
- ♥ 1 cup hot water
- ♥ 1 pound cottage cheese
- ♥ 1 large can pet milk
- ♥ 1 cup mayonnaise
- ♥ 1 large can crushed pineapple
- ♥ ¾ cup pecan pieces

Dissolve the 2 packages of Jell-O in hot water.

Stir well.

Add all other ingredients.

Pour in an 8-cup mold and chill.

Mind Snacks!
♥ He that falls in love with himself, will have no rivals.
♥ I like the dreams of the future better than the history of the past. *(Thomas Jefferson)*
♥ Silence is not only golden; It's seldom misquoted.

Green & White Salad

Beautiful to serve and delicious!

- ♥ 1 - 3 ounce package lime Jell-O
- ♥ 1 cup boiling water
- ♥ 1 can crushed pineapple
- ♥ 1 package cream cheese
- ♥ 1 - 3 ounce package lemon Jell-O
- ♥ 1 cup boiling water
- ♥ 1 cup half & half cream (whipped)

Dissolve lime Jell-O in 1 cup boiling water and let cool.

Add pineapple and chill.

Dissolve lemon Jell-O in 1 cup boiling water and let cool.

Combine whipped cream and cream cheese and add to lemon Jell-O.

Pour over lime Jell-O mixture and chill.

Mind Snacks!

- ♥ Just because tomorrow is another day is no reason to waste this one.

- ♥ Remember, in every lease the big print giveth and the small print taketh away.

- ♥ It takes less time to do a thing right than it does to explain why you did it wrong. (*Henry W Longfellow*)

- ♥ Some people's idea of free speech is that they are free to say what they like, but if anyone says anything back, that is an outrage. (*Winston Churchill*)

Mama Quisenberry's Slaw

An old favorite from my grandmother.

- ♥ Head of cabbage
- ♥ Tablespoon sugar
- ♥ One egg
- ♥ ½ cup vinegar

Cut up the cabbage and sprinkle with sugar.

Beat the egg well.

Heat the vinegar in a skillet and pour in the beaten egg and stir until thick.

Pour mixture over cabbage.

Peggy's Cole Slaw

- ♥ 2 cups cabbage, sliced thin
- ♥ 1 Golden delicious apple, diced
- ♥ 1 small carrot, diced
- ♥ 1 teaspoon sugar
- ♥ 1 cup white raisins, optional

Dressing:

Mix 1 tablespoon mayonnaise with

　1 tablespoon Kraft's Cole Slaw dressing.

Serves about 4 people

A Visit From Donna & Paul's Children

Tori, Karen, and Justin came to visit for a week while their parents vacationed in Hawaii. Every other day I would take them somewhere exciting, like Disneyland, the San Diego Zoo, and Universal Studios. Then on alternate days we would stay home and swim, play tennis and other games.

One day towards the end of the week, they became restless. I suggested we walk to the mall, about two miles away, and look around. Then we would call Granddad and have him pick us up and we would eat out. This was greeted with, "Yes, let's go."

Before long Karen got tired and wanted me to carry her. She was 6 years old! She lagged behind and whined and complained every step of the way. When we got closer to the mall, I said, "Let's go by City Hall, Sometimes exciting things happen there."

We were in luck! They were filming a TV show. Sitting in front of the building were Kirk Cameron and a reporter. We stood behind the reporter and watched Kirk being interviewed. At the time he was probably seventeen years old. He began flirting with Karen.

After the interview, Kirk took her by the hand and said, "Would you like to go inside and see what we are doing?" She said yes, with her eyes shining!. He turned to me as if to say is it all right? I gave my OK.

We waited outside for about ten minutes, when he came back out with Karen and approached us, the other two kids watching very jealously.

Karen's exact words were, "Oh Grandmom, I'll never complain again when you want me to walk somewhere!" Never, never, never, ever.

Thank you Kirk for taking the time to make a little six year old so very happy!

Pea Salad

If you like peas, you'll love this one!

- ♥ 2 cups lettuce (shredded)
- ♥ 1 package frozen peas (cooked as directed on package)
- ♥ 1 small onion (chopped)
- ♥ 10 slices of bacon (fried crisp and crumbled)
- ♥ 1 cup parmesan cheese
- ♥ 1 cup mayonnaise

Mix together first 3 ingredients with mayonnaise.

Mix bacon and cheese and sprinkle on top.

Serve over lettuce mixture.

Mind Snacks!

♥ *Jellinek's disease (alcoholism) is responsible for:*

—50 percent of all auto fatalities

-80 percent of all home violence

-30 percent of all suicides

-60 percent of all child abuse

-65 percent of all drowning

It is estimated that when a woman contracts the disease, her husband leaves her in nine out of ten cases; when a man contracts it his wife leaves in one out of ten cases. (*Kathleen W Fitzgerald*)

Poppy Seed Dressing for Fruit

Really an excellent topping for fruit snacks!

- ½ cup vinegar
- 1 cup sugar
- 1 teaspoon salt
- 2 teaspoons dry mustard
- 2 cups Wesson oil
- 1 small onion (grated)
- 2 tablespoons poppy seeds
- red food coloring

Mix sugar, salt, mustard, and vinegar.

Add oil gradually.

Beat until thick.

Add onion, poppy seeds, and one or two drops of food coloring.

Store in air tight container in refrigerator.

To serve: pour over your choice of cut-up fruits.

Mind Snacks!

- Minutes at the table don't put on weight - it's the seconds.
- If you cheat on your diet - you gain in the end.
- A man who is his own doctor has a fool for his patient.

Soups

Donna's Chili

The very best chili you ever ate.

- ♥ 2 pounds ground beef (browned)
- ♥ 1 medium onion (diced)
- ♥ 1 can tomato sauce
- ♥ 2 packages chili mix
- ♥ 1 can tomato soup.
- ♥ 1 can chili beans
- ♥ 1 can red beans
- ♥ 1 can beer
- ♥ ½ package sharp cheddar cheese (grated)
- ♥ chili powder (to taste)
- ♥ 1 red pepper (diced)
- ♥ salt & pepper (to taste)

Mix all ingredients except the cheese.

Simmer for 2 hours.

Serve over fresh corn bread and sprinkle with grated cheese & extra onions if you like.

Mind Snacks!

♥ I went on a fourteen-day diet, but all I lost was two weeks.

Peel-A-Pound Soup

Diet soup!

- ♥ 1 bunch of celery (diced)
- ♥ 1 green pepper (diced)
- ♥ 1 red pepper (diced)
- ♥ 1 head cabbage (cut up)
- ♥ 2 large onions (diced)
- ♥ 2 large potatoes (cut up)
- ♥ 2 carrots (diced)
- ♥ 1 pound can tomatoes
- ♥ 2 packages dry onion soup mix
- ♥ 1 bouillon cube
- ♥ Add water to taste (thick or thin)

Simmer all ingredients for 2 hours. You can eat as much as you want without gaining weight.

Mind Snacks!

♥ The difficulties of life are intended to make us better, not bitter.

♥ Never underestimate the power of a kind word or deed.

♥ Whistle a happy tune and watch faces light up.

Our Continuing Story!

When our family was still young Vic and I decided that we would always make a special effort to see that our family did not drift apart. Over the years our family has become spread out all across the country and for that matter the globe (Australia & New Zealand), but we have not drifted apart.

We resolved that at the very least we would always get the family together for an extended visit at Christmas. Our strategy to accomplish this was not to "nag" the family, but to make each Christmas different and "special".

Each year we plan a special adventure that the entire family looks forward too. Also, Vic and I are determined to remain truly "alive" and active and do exciting things together with our family.

We have had tremendous adventures together and made memories that are very special.

Among our many adventures some of our most special are:

- ♥ Road trip through southern California including: Leggo Land, the Wild Animal Park, El Centro, Mexico, and the Center of the World in Felicity, California.
- ♥ Road trip through Arizona: Gorgeous Sedona, Cottonwood, Jerome, and a Helicopter trip through the Grand Canyon.
- ♥ A wonderful snowmobile adventure in Yellowstone Park.
- ♥ Hot air ballooning in southern California.

In our adventures many of our most special memories are not the big exciting events, but the memories of sitting together playing cards and laughing (and occasionally fussing) together. Sometimes in a mountain chalet overlooking Yellowstone, sometimes in a motel room in El Centro California or Cottonwood Arizona.

It really doesn't matter where, as long as you are together with your family, both physically and spiritually. Cherish your lives and your families. They are both special and they don't last forever!

Cooking Aids and Reminders

Cooking is really an art.

It takes time and patience, and of course an understanding of common terms, measures, and practices.

Following are some standards you may need to refer to from time to time.

These are also very helpful to the inexperienced and infrequent culinary wizards in your home!

Cooking Terms

Baste: To moisten with liquid during cooking, using a spoon or bulb baster, most often for oven and pot roasts and broiled meats or fish.

Bind: To thicken the liquid of a soup, gravy or stew with a starch such as flour or cornstarch, or with egg yolks.

Blanch: To place in boiling water for a given amount of time and then cold water, for the purposes of partially cooking or peeling.

Blend: To combine ingredients of different textures such as butter and sugar - a gentler mixing than beating.

Braise: To sear or brown in fat, then cook slowly, covered, with a minimum of liquid, on stove or in oven.

Breading: A coating of flour and/or breadcrumbs used on foods that are to be fried. Beaten egg or milk may be used to help coating adhere.

Coat a Spoon: Custards and sauces which contain egg yolk or cornstarch must often cook until they are thick enough to leave a coating on a spoon, indicating their degree of doneness.

Cut and Fold: To gently combine a lighter mixture such as beaten egg whites with a heavier mixture such as a cream sauce or cake batter. To do this, place heavier mixture over lighter, cut down through middle of both with a rubber spatula and draw spatula toward you, turning mixture over as you do so. Continue around the bowl in this fashion.

Flambe': Heated brandy (or other spirits) is poured over cooked or partially cooked food and is then ignited and allowed to burn off.

Julienne: Food is cut into very thin, long matchstick strips.

Knead: To work dough by pushing it with the heel of your hand, folding it over and repeating until it has reached degree of smoothness indicated in recipe.

Lard: To run strips of fat (bacon or lard) through meat or fish to keep it moist during cooking - usually done with a larding needle.

Marinate: To soak food, usually meat or fish, in a liquid that will add to its flavor or make it more tender.

Roux: A mixture of fat and flour sautéed together and then added to liquid to thicken it.

Skim: To remove fat from top of soups, stews or pan gravies after it has risen - a spoon or bulb baster is best for this. Easiest way to do thorough skimming job is to chill liquid until fat solidifies at the top.

Steam: To cook in steam (usually fish or vegetable) by placing food in a covered, perforated container over boiling water. Usually an alternate to boiling, steaming takes much longer, but preserves flavor and vitamins.

155

Roasting Chart

Meat	Oven Temperature (degrees)	Internal Temperature	Time Per Pound	
			Weight of Meat - pounds	Cooking Time - min.
Beef	300 to 325	Rare - 140 Med. - 160 Well - 170	6 to 8	18 to 20 22 to 25 27 to 30
Pork, Fresh	350	185	3 to 7	35 to 45
Ham, Precooked	300 to 325	130	10 to 12	12 to 15
Ham, Smoked uncooked	300 to 325	160	10 to 14	18 to 20
Lamb	300 to 325	170 to 185	3 to 5	30 to 35
Veal	300	170	5 to 8	25 -30
Meat	**Oven Temperature (degrees)**	**Internal Temperature**	**Weight of Meat pounds**	**Cooking Time hours**
Turkey	325	190	10 to 14	4 to 5
Chicken	375	190	4 to 6	2 ½ to 3 ½
Duckling	325	190	4 to 5	2 to 3
Capon	325 to 350	190	6 to 8	2 ½ to 3 ½
Goose	325	190	10 to 12	4 to 5

How Much and How Many

Butter, Chocolate

- ♥ 2 tablespoons butter = 1 ounce
- ♥ 1 stick or ¼ pound butter = ½ cup
- ♥ 1 square chocolate = 1 ounce

Crumbs

- ♥ 20 salted crackers = 1 cup fine crumbs
- ♥ 12 graham crackers = 1 cup fine crumbs
- ♥ 22 vanilla wafers = 1 cup fine crumbs
- ♥ 8 to 9 slices zwieback = 1 cup fine crumbs
- ♥ 1 slice bread = ½ cup soft crumbs

Cereals

- ♥ 4 ounces macaroni (1 - 1 ¼ cups) = 2 ¼ cups cooked
- ♥ 4 ounces noodles (1 ½ - 2 cups) = 2 ¼ cups cooked
- ♥ 4 ounces spaghetti (1 - 1 ¼ cups) = 2 ½ cups cooked
- ♥ 1 cup uncooked rice (6 ½ - 7 ounces) = 3 - 3 ½ cups cooked
- ♥ 1 cup precooked rice = 2 cups cooked

Fruits, Vegetables

- ♥ Juice of 1 lemon = 3 - 4 tablespoons
- ♥ Grated peel of lemon = 1 teaspoon
- ♥ Juice of 1 orange = 6 - 7 tablespoons
- ♥ Grated peel of 1 orange = about 2 teaspoons
- ♥ 1 medium apple, chopped = 1 cup
- ♥ 1 medium onion, chopped = ½ cup
- ♥ ¼ pound celery (about 2 stalks), chopped = 1 cup

Cheese and Eggs

- ♥ 1 pound process cheese, shredded = 4 cups

- ¼ pound blue cheese, crumbled = ¾ to 1 cup
- 12 to 14 egg yolks = 1 cup
- 8 to 10 egg whites = 1 cup

Nuts

- 1 pound walnuts in shell = 2 cups, shelled
- ¼ pound chopped walnuts = about 1 cup
- 1 pound almonds in shell = about 1 cup, shelled

Herbs and Spices

ALLSPICE
- Pickling, liver pate', ginger bread, holiday baking, pork and ham, pumpkin and squash dishes.

ANISE
- Cakes, cookies, breads.

BASIL
- Italian dishes, vegetables, meats, tomato salads and sauces.

BAY LEAVES
- Grilled fish, marinades, meat stews and soups.

CARDAMOM
- Widely used in Indian curries as well as in Scandinavian Christmas breads and cookies, stewed fruits and grape jelly.

CAYENNE PEPPER
- Egg dishes, salads dressing, cream sauces, cottage cheese dips.

CHERVIL
- Egg dishes, salad dressings, cream sauces, cottage cheese dips.

CHIVES
- ♥ Fresh or dried are excellent in dips, salads, garnishing for potatoes and soups - steep dried chives in hot water 15 minutes before using.

CINNAMON
- ♥ Toast, tea, cocoa, fruit desserts and pies, rice pudding, Middle Eastern meat and rice dishes.

CLOVES
- ♥ Ham, apple desserts, spiced tea, tomato bouillon, creamed onions.

CURRY POWDER
- ♥ Mayonnaise or cream sauces for fish, lamb, poultry.

DILL
- ♥ Cucumber salads, salmon, sauce for boiled bee, chicken, or fish.

GARLIC
- ♥ Used mostly in French, Italian, Spanish and Chinese recipes. Excellent with lamb, shellfish, in salad dressings and appetizer dips. Garlic salt or powder should be used only when fresh garlic is not available.

GINGER
- ♥ Broiled chicken, pot roasts, peach desserts, fish sauces, barbecues, holiday baking.

MARJORAM
- ♥ Meat stews and soups, dried beans and peas.

MINT
- ♥ Use fresh or dried mint to flavor sauce for lamb, and fresh sprigs in cold drinks, salads, peas and pea soup and Middle Eastern yogurt sauces.

NUTMEG
♥ Rice and sweet puddings, eggnog, spinach, mushrooms, wild rice, cauliflower.

OREGANO
♥ Meat and poultry roasts and stews, vegetable casseroles, Italian sauces.

PAPRIKA
♥ Meat and poultry goulashes, broiled fish, rarebits, decorative topping.

ROSEMARY
♥ Lamb, veal, poultry.

SAFFRON
♥ Risotto, pilaff, paella, Swedish coffee cake, bouillabaisse.

SAGE
♥ Pork, poultry or onion stuffings, sausage meat.

SAVORY
♥ String beans, cabbage, salad dressing, dried peas and beans.

TARRAGON
♥ Green mayonnaise for fish, Béarnaise sauce, roasted poultry, salads and dressings.

THYME
♥ Clam chowder, meat and vegetable soups and stews, egg dishes.

Weights and Measures

3 teaspoons equal 1 tablespoon	1 cup equals 8 fluid ounces
2 tablespoons equal 1/8 cup	1 cup equals 1/2 pint
4 tablespoons equal 1/4 cup	2 cups equal 1 pint
5 1/3 tablespoons equal 1/3 cup	4 cups equal 1 quart
8 tablespoons equal 1/2 cup	4 quarts equal 1 gallon
10 2/3 tablespoons equal 2/3 cup	8 quarts equal 1 peck
12 tablespoons equal 3/4 cup	4 pecks equal 1 bushel
14 tablespoons equal 7/8 cup	
16 tablespoons equal 1 cup	

Our Wedding 1950   25th Anniversary 1975   50th Anniversary - Aruba

Our Family in 1964   Grandchildren - Justin, Karen, Tori, Ashley & Victor IV

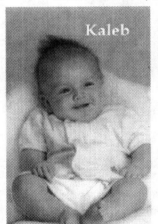
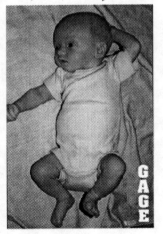

Recent Arrivals - Grandson Michael & Great Grandsons Kaleb & Gage

Our Children

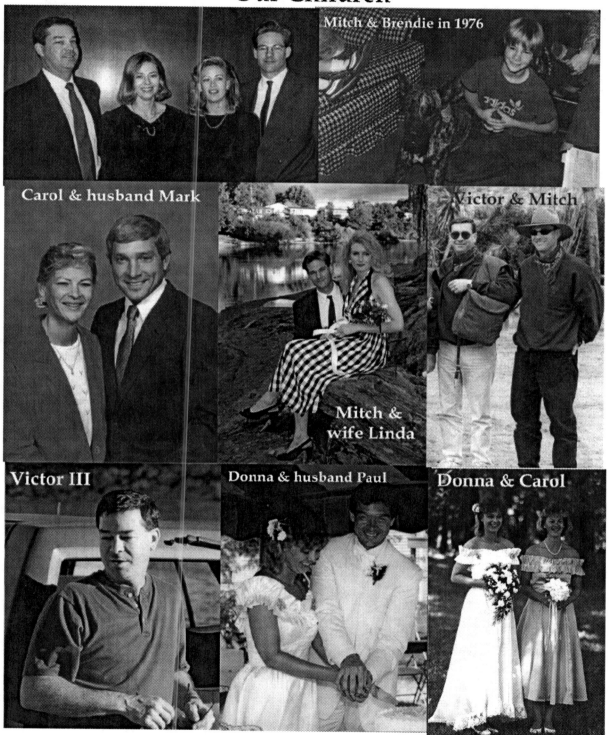

Mitch & Brendie in 1976

Carol & husband Mark

Victor & Mitch

Mitch & wife Linda

Victor III

Donna & husband Paul

Donna & Carol

Our Ham Shop in Monrovia, Ca

Peggy Love in Ham Shop she ran

Playing Cards (Hand & Foot)

At the original Angel's ballpark

Helicopter Ride at Grand Canyon

Desert Jeep Adventure

Ogden Ranch,
Cottonwood Arizona

My Granddaughter
Tori's Wedding

Snowmobiling
Yellowstone Park

Flying Gliders
Hemet California

Aruba - 50th Anniversary

Horseback Riding
Palm Springs, Cal.

Have Fun While You Cook!

About the Author

The author, Peggy Love (Anderson), is a housewife, former business owner / operator, world traveler, Bridge Life-Master, and mother of four.

This is her second published book. Peggy's first book "It's No Secret Anymore," is based on the true story of Ursula Kanel, a friend of the author's. This book is a collection of recipes and many short stories involving family members.

Peggy Love loves to tell stories of her life and both her books reveal this. She lives with her husband of fifty years, Vic, in Walnut, California.

Printed in the United States
93403LV00003B/51-110/A